This book is dedicated to the people who live on the Great Plains.

People of the Great Plains

© 1996 Peter Miller

All rights reserved. No parts of the contents of
this book may be reproduced by any means without
the written permission of the publisher.

Published by Silver Print Press
Route 100, RD 1, Box 1515, Waterbury, Vt. 05676
802-244-5339

Book Design by Peter Holm

Edited by Hilary Miller

Library of Congress Catalog Card Number: 96-69119

Printed in the United States of America by The Stinehour Press

First Edition

Books by Peter Miller: *The 30,000 Mile Ski Race, Peter Miller's Ski Almanac,
The Photographer's Almanac* (co-author), *Vermont People*

Publisher's – Cataloging In Publication
Miller, Peter. People of the Great Plains.
Documentary photos and text on people and scenery of the Great Plains.
176 p.
ISBN: 0-9628064-2-0
1. Great Plains — Description and travel —1981-
2. West(U.S.) — Description and travel — 1981-
3. Great Plains — Social life and customs.
4. Miller, Peter — Journey — People of the Great Plains.
F595.3.M.55 1996   978.033

People of the Great Plains has been generously supported by:

The Countryside Institute
TCI was founded in 1990 to find ways of conserving America's countryside,
while enhancing the lives of people and communities.

The Image Bank Award for Visual Excellence
The Image Bank is a wholly-owned subsidiary of the Eastman Kodak Company. With over
70 offices in more than 35 countries, it represents the work of photographers, illustrators and
cinematographers and provides their imagery to clients for print and broadcast advertising,
as well as promotional and editorial use.

Grateful acknowledgment is made to the following for
permission to reproduce photographs and reprint previously published material:

Page 22-23: Photos courtesy Helen Blomquist Kramer
Page 48: excerpts from *From The Deep Plains* newsletter © 1996 Lawrence Brown
Page 78: Medicine Wheel illustration © 1996 Narcisse Heart
Page 98: excerpts from *No Time But Place, A Prairie Pastoral*, by Jeff and Jessica
    Pearson, © 1980 McGraw Hill and San Francisco Book Company.
Page 98: Plowing Photo. Credit: Seward County Historical Society, Liberal, Kansas.
Page 138: Elephant Saloon photo. Credit: Western History Collections, University of
    Oklahoma Library.
Page 148: "Roundup In The Spring". Original poem by Carl Copeland and Jack Williams.
    J.B. Allen's version available on tape, Box 68, Whiteface, TX 79379
Page 162: Charlie Goodnight photo © 1996 Andy Wilkinson
Page 164: "Prairie Without Buffalo" and "The Last Buffalo Hunt"
    © 1996 Andy Wilkinson. *Cain't Quit Music*, Inc./BMI, 5205 92nd St. Lubbock, Tx 79424.
    All rights reserved. Used by permission.
Page 166: Photo by Skye Chalmers

People of the Great Plains

PETER MILLER

Silver Print Press
1996

More than twenty-five major publishers rejected this book. One editor in New York asked why I was doing a book on Iowa. To coastal Americans, the Plains really is fly-over country.

Most people who study this region say the Great Plains begins at the 98th meridian at 1,500 feet elevation and ends at about 6,000 feet at the bottom of the Rockies. The 98th slices down the center of North and South Dakota, Nebraska, the western sections of Kansas and Oklahoma and into Texas. Drive 100 miles west of the 98th and the trees are replaced by buffalo grass, the humidity is squeezed from the air and the light is pure and sharp. Other names for the region are the High Plains and the Short Grass Plains.

The Great Plains stretches from Saskatchewan, Canada and ends at the southern edge of the Staked Plains in the Texas Panhandle.

The Plains is not only flat, it is dry. In Lincoln, Nebraska, which is more prairie than Plains, the annual rainfall is 26 inches. Most of the Plains near the 100th meridian, where I photographed, receives under 20 inches of rain, the minimum amount of rain to sustain agriculture unaided by irrigation. A sustainable farm or ranch is rarely under 2,000 acres.

Because the Plains is flat, treeless and dry, it was called (in the 1830s and 1840s) The Great American Desert, although, at the time, it supported 50 Indian tribes and 60 million buffalo.

Trappers were the first to infiltrate the region. They were followed by pioneers heading to the western coast, and cattlemen and sheep herders. Railroads transported homesteaders and barbed wire closed off the open range.

Population and economy fluctuated with the extremes of weather. The blizzard of 1886 ended the era of cattle barons. Drought then settled in for a decade; in 1891, 18,000 retreating prairie schooners entered Iowa from Nebraska.

Rain in the early 1900s brought hope and more homesteaders. Mechanized farming and drought created the Dirty Thirties – the Dust Bowl and its swarms of hungry locusts, and hungry people. It collided with the Great Depression and another forlorn migration of refugees began.

Wheat became a muscle crop in the late forties and early fifties. Drought returned in the late eighties. Rain has brought succor to the northern Plains but the drought is the worst recorded in the southern Plains from Kansas and Nebraska to Texas and New Mexico.

The history of the Plains is hardship and suffering, bankruptcy, tragedy, waste and extermination. Whites battled Indians and killed buffalo, cattle ranchers fought sheep herders and farmers. The horse and the six shooter opened the west and the railroad settled it. This half century of growth and change was played against suffocating heat waves, wind-screaming winters, deadly blizzards, lightning-lit grass fires, cloudbursts and hail bigger than golf balls, tornadoes, sand and dust storms.

Still, the Plains is rich enough to overfeed America with grain and meat. The Ogallala aquifer that extends from Nebraska to Texas is the main source of water. It is a blessing and a curse. The aquifer is now tapped by so many wells the land may lose the ability to replenish itself.

Families who remain on these steppes, and each year there are fewer of them, have toughed it out and often live on land owned or homesteaded by their ancestors. They love their freedom. They are stubborn, but resilient, skilled and innovative – arid regions have always produced these qualities in people.

The Great Plains is the glue between the east and west of our country. This fly-over land supports people of moral strength and goodness of heart, almost forgotten traits in Americans. They retain in their character the history of our country and of their tribes. The region in which they live reflects the best and worst of our historical soul.

People of the Great Plains

On a muggy afternoon of the summer solstice, 1993, I hitched a tiny Airstream camper to my Jeep and set off from Vermont on a journey to the Plains. I was not sure where I was going or how long I would stay. All I knew is that I wanted to photograph and write about the Plains and its people.

Why? I am not sure. I was curious. I have no roots there but I thought the people would be like Vermonters. Perhaps it was a quest to learn, with the Plains as my teacher, about myself. And, as any traveling journalist will tell you, we are happiest in the field, seeing new places, meeting people.

In three years I made four trips to the Plains and drove 30,000 miles. I can recall, vividly, each day of those seven months. Below are excerpts from my journal.

Arnold, Nebraska. These people are farmers. They are having Sunday dinner in the Model Cafe, seated next to a glass cabinet loaded with tall wedges of lemon chiffon and rhubarb pie – babies to 80-year-olds. The old farmers move with slow, deliberate movements, the measured movements of their life. The faces are wrinkled, the smiles are open. There must be something to hold these people to these large, flat

cornfields, with only the clouds above for a view. Is it family, community, or just fate?

Arthur, Nebraska. Freedom! The land is open. The wind is brisk and the temperature cool. The humidity is gone. I am in the west, in the Sand Hills. Nothing but grass and rolling hills. So few trees, so few people. This is truly an ocean; a hill is a wave and about every fifth hill is bigger and on the other side are more waves. It extends to South Dakota and towards Kansas. The wind blows constantly, rippling the grass. If I were a sailboat, I would surf from wave to wave...

I am parked in an empty fairgrounds and exposing my bleached body to the sun. This, of course, is blasphemous out here, where most everyone is a rancher or cowboy. They cover up against the sun and never take off their cowboy hats. If they do, a white band extends up to the hairline. If the cowboy is bald, it circles his forehead, the equator of the face.

Hyannis, Nebraska. My mind sometimes turns inward, to the route that led here, a route of the mind, of circumstances I do not control. There is something about traveling alone that brings forth thoughts of life past, of people who have been loved and not loved, of friends lost by place and time or misunderstanding, of tiny moments shared that brought happiness and sometimes hurt. I see a simpler life here, not complicated by the deviations of life as I have lived it….There are no shadows in the mid-day sun and no verticals in this landscape.

Ashby, Nebraska. A lesson about these people – I stopped in at the Adams home and we had a chat.

"Hear about the man hanging from the windmill by his foot?"

"No!"

"Why a woman drove by this windmill not far from Hyannis and this man is hanging from it by his foot. She reported it to the gas station in Hyannis and they went up and he was dead. Well, he was a big man, about 280 pounds but he was tall, too. He had a brace on his hip.

"It wasn't too smart but that was his little spread and he had some longhorn cattle and what else are you supposed to do if your windmill doesn't work? You can't get help, you know."

Near Sand Springs, Montana. This is a land of immense aloneness and not loneliness. These people have dedicated their life to hard work. They know nothing else, they say. I've been here all my life, they say. They know where their roots are. Many have hobbies to carry them over the winter. They are rooted to the environment, not as free as the antelope but not as fenced in as cattle.

Capulin, New Mexico. Clarity and purity of light expands these Plains. Grass, stone, flowers are defined by details, each a jewel. It is like looking through a microscope. I savor the tones and shades in shards of shale and clumps of mesquite. There is drastic contrast between direct sun and shadows, which are black and unfathomable. Perhaps this is why western photographers use big cameras to capture such fine detail. Distances are shortened, human structures are intrusions – barbed wire fences, a column of power lines, an old rutted trail, covered with grass and softened by winds.

Clareton, Wyoming. There is a feeling of people, the lack of people, the want for people, the desire for no people. I want to draw the horizons into my soul and have them bounce around so much that they expand my horizons and I become unfettered. This is a metaphysical land.

Lemmon, South Dakota. Some of the small things that make the difference between the east and the Plains: strike anywhere matches, volatile charcoal lighter fluid, 20 ounce cans of "pop" for 65 cents, watermelon served with salt, hail-smashed windshields, antique threshing machines posed on hills as works of art, Minuteman missile sites, some of them recently dug up, stink of cattle that wafts behind the trucks they are transported in, a cow with its head cut off on the side of the road, rattlesnakes popped by tires in the middle of the road, a cowboy grazing his horse in the median of an interstate highway.

Near Liberal, Kansas. A black squall is heading my way, very fast, then is upon me. Huge drops of rain splatter, then *pow*, hail smashes on my car and ricochets off. They are as big as marble agates. The wind becomes fierce. I turn the car away from the storm, holy God, they are now as big as golf balls and I put on the wipers. The hail explodes on the roof like rifle shots and shreds leaves from the cottonwood where I am parked, the only tree near this road. In 15 minutes the storm is over, in 20 minutes the white agates of hail have melted.

Slim Buttes, South Dakota. A north wind is blowing the snow horizontally in gusts of about 40 to 50 miles per hour. I don't know what the temperature is, but I have put on my face mask. There are whiteouts in the distance from the bluff where I am standing. The wind hums and invades my heavy down parka and down vest and heavy wool pants and long johns and sneaks into every little opening. I understand why ranchers wear one-piece zip-up suits. Five inches of snow have stuck to the ground but the rest appears to be blowing to Vermont. This is a killing wind for the unprepared; it could suck the life right out of you. It is a gale in the middle of the sea and I'm not sure whether this storm in this immense land makes me bigger in spirit, or smaller. At times I realize how inconsequential we all are, isolated souls. Then I become part of this storm, part of a circle of weather so strong time seems to subside.

Palo Duro Canyon, Texas to Tucumcari, New Mexico. I never knew such heat. It is 107 degrees and I don't sweat. I drink water and eat fruit and suffer because, being from a cold state, I don't have air conditioning in my car or in the camper. I am living in a convection oven and this heat desiccates my mind and body. I cannot sleep and the next day I leave the canyon early, unlatching the hood of my car and turning on the heater, so the engine will not overheat. Driving on I-40, the sun coats the road and landscape a pale yellow. Cars that pass glisten and shine. The heat envelopes me, pounds me, burns my body and brain, pinches my nostrils – the same as frigid weather, when the air is dry and the temperature drops to zero. On the interstate all is flat and hot, I am in the center of a burning circle that is crimped by the horizon. There is a dome over my head and the pull of gravity under my feet and nothing else, nothing else in the world. The horizon is incandescent in a sheen of heat. My eyes squint into slits as my sunglasses are not strong enough. My stomach cramps. This heat could be an hallucinogenic drug. I see an 18-wheeler parked at the Texas-New Mexico border that has lettered on it Batesville Casket Company. Ha! If I died here, I wouldn't need a casket, I would just dry up and blow away.

South Dakota, on Route 212 to the Cheyenne River Reservation. Time can't be measured here, perhaps because the landscape is timeless. This road is time, measured in telephone poles and miles. There is no time in my life and death, only continuity. Time is forever, time is nothing. I am part of the grass and sky, for this is the community of the Plains. Ones lives here to an eternal clock. What is time to the wind, the sun, a horse or the buffalo, the color of winter, the color of grass, or the heat of the sun on my body? What is time to a teepee ring? Time is the past and future and time is nothing. Where does the soul fit here? Why are people here? Why am I here? Overhead one cloud is in the sky and I am under its shadow. Still, the brightness burns my eyes.

Fred Dubray, Cheyenne River Reservation:

"You say we are caught in the past but it is the other way around. You Europeans consider yourselves above plants and animals with only God above you. Because you see yourself as superior, you destroy habitat and animals and then destroy yourselves. We say, 'All My Relatives'. Everything is related and we are all in this together because we are all dependent upon each other."

Merle Clark, Marmarth, North Dakota:

"One of my ancestors walked here from Dickinson. He brought 50 pounds of flour, a Kentucky rifle and axes, and built a log cabin. We never left. We're stubborn. We stick it out while others leave, but we sure hate to lose a neighbor. I hear people back in cities don't know their neighbors. I would be ashamed."

Jim Rosebery, newspaper editor, Boise City News, Oklahoma:

"I wish I was anonymous so I could report what people do not want reported, but if I do, things happen to me, my wife, my kids. It is like being black. Still, I love this area where people from other parts crinkle their brows when I say where I am from. This land is sad and happy. Relaxed and sad. It is an existential land. It is metaphysical. It sings to me like Pachelbel's Canon in D. I like it a lot."

Brother Placid, Benedictine Monk, Richardton, North Dakota:

"Why do you take so many pictures? It makes stress. Just take one and you do not have to choose. Make life easier."

Young Man Afraid of his Horses, Pine Ridge Reservation:

"It is the Lakota way not to talk bad about people and not be negative. We talk about the good things in people. There must be forgiveness for everybody....We do everything day by day. When I wake up I pray for tomorrow. I give thanks for yesterday and I pray that everything will be good this day."

Margaret Hawkins, Arthur, Nebraska, when she asked me where I was headed and I replied that I did not know:

"You remind me of what my Daddy said. He told me about the goofus bird that flies backwards. It always knows where it has been but not where it's going."

**Thoughts to myself,
driving from the Plains east,
into a land of trees and population and stress:**

I have located the excess baggage I am carrying from the past that I should leave behind. I learned that time and the hardships of weather soften human arrogance. I gained an extended family, for I now realize that my family includes everyone I photograph. The Plains taught me about an interior freedom.

I was 59 when I started this quest and, after all those years, I have learned to take responsibility for my talents. And I am a goofus bird. I like to know where I have been, but not necessarily where I am going...

Peter Miller

People of the Great Plains

Montana

Wheat, nothing but wheat. Stripes of gold, stripes of brown. Fallow earth and hard winter red wheat stretch to faint bumps of mountains swelling on the horizon. Puff clouds, scattered under a sky deep in blue as the South Pacific, sail towards the east. A slight wind cools the sun this August day on the 111th meridian, 80 miles east of the Rockies, 25 miles west of High Butte. Some call this the Golden Triangle, an area centered around Carter, a town too easy to miss between Great Falls and Fort Benton.

Five miles east of Carter, in a school yard plunked next to a crossroads, the Walter Custom Harvesting crew has set up camp. They are from a farm in Alberta, Canada, just across the Montana border. Most of the Walter crew are Mennonites. Ben Walter runs the operation, his wife Donna is the camp boss and cook and is helped by her daughter Lynore, who drives a combine and is proud that she is as good a driver as any of the guys.

Ben is a calm, handsome man who talks thoughtfully and looks as though there is no such thing as stress to harvesting 60,000 acres of wheat, barley and canola in a season. He never loses his temper, never shows frustration at bad weather or wheat that destroys his timetable because it is not quite ripe.

The Walter crew came down in July to Colorado and are working their way home. They have 12 Case and John Deere combines that together can cut a 300 foot swatch through a crop field, do-si-do with each other at the corners and gracefully return to the other side. At the end of a work day, the crew can place up to 65,000 bushels of winter red in a grain elevator.

The wheat whacking crew – that is what they call themselves – spend up to 20 hours a day in their air-conditioned tractor cabins. Mennonites are not supposed to listen to popular music but every so often that music is heard on the CBs in their cab. "Hey, what's that noise I hear?" one driver will say over the CB to his combine partner to the rear and the answer is a laugh.

"The business is tricky," says Ben, taking off his cap to wipe his brow, his black hair matted flat with sweat. "A wind storm can knock a farmer's crop flat and he loses 40% of his income. Grain can be ripe in one farmer's field and 10 miles away

it is not ready. The moisture content may be too high or a rainstorm cuts apart a tight schedule."

Ben speaks in an even tempo, tuned with a slight German accent overlaying a Canadian cadence.

"You know," Ben continues, "the price of wheat is not going up. A combine in 1979 cost about $80,000 in Canadian dollars; now it is about $160,000 and the new machines are only 10% more efficient than ten years ago. We charge the same as we did five, seven years ago. Volume, everything is volume. This is a game, you know, but I like the challenge. It is exhilarating to pull into a crop of wheat three, four feet high and cut it."

Ben and his crew are cutting the crops of Richard and Berta Robinson, who own a 2,000 acre farm, one of the smallest in Carter. The Robinsons live in a ranch house protected from the wind by a row of Russian olive trees backed by red pine. A colorful garden and a tiny greenhouse overstuffed with ripening tomatoes and cucumbers brighten their home.

The Robinsons are wheat and barley farmers and are the third generation to work this land. Berta is an attractive woman who speaks her mind. Richard is more introspective with a finely lined face, a tattoo on his arm and kind, blue eyes. This couple seem to enjoy each other.

"Farming," says Richard, "it has its ups and downs."

"Mostly downs," adds Berta, and then both of them open up while their black cat sitting on the couch pays no attention whatsoever.

"It's water and grain prices. Last year it rained all summer and that was a disaster. We had Federal crop insurance and everyone thinks it is free but we pay for it," says Richard.

"Price of wheat stays the same and everything else goes up," continues Berta. "In 1950 the price of wheat was $2.25 a bushel and the cost of a car was $1,700. Now wheat is $3.50 a bushel and the car is over $20,000. We only buy used tractors. Fuel and fertilizer and repairs are all up, and then people blame us for ruining the environment. Why, the county sprays more fertilizers on the road than we use on the fields."

They both lament the coming of bigger farms, bigger cars and better roads. Before they had dances, box socials and card parties. Now everyone who has not sold out and moved away drives to Great Falls for their social life. They also find they are working harder and don't have time to take Sunday off (Now they do. The Robinsons recently retired to the mountains and left the farming to their children. "They need the experience," says Berta.)

Not all the wheat ends up in bins on farms. Much of it is trucked to the Peavey grain elevator in Carter. The elevator is owned by ConAgra of Omaha, Nebraska, one of the largest agriculture companies in the world. About four million bushels of grain go in and out of the Carter elevators during an average year.

J.B. Walker is in charge. His grandfather, cousins and uncles have all worked in grain elevators and he calls it a family tradition. When the wheat is trucked in he measures it for protein, how much chaff is mixed in and prices it and logs on the computer the amount. The trains arrive on Wednesday, fill up and head for the west coast. J.B. assumes most of the grain is turned into noodles in Japan.

J.B., in his off time, likes to hunt. He says that running a grain elevator is not good for longevity and causes problems with lungs.

"Well, one operator lived to be 82 but I know of five who retired and died within a year. I don't know, dust or drinking, well, we're up here in the boonies."

Six miles to the west the Walter crew finishes cutting the Robinson fields. Two mule tail does browse nonchalantly in a grass field blocked by a dirt road from the combines. Blond chaff puffs and scatters behind them and the whine of engines drifts slowly up a bluff. It is like slow motion line dancing as combines and grain carts move up and down the rectangular patches.

Later in the afternoon, a Saturday, a young woman, slim and graceful in her long dress, greets her husband; the crew quit early. The couple walks down the middle of the gravel road from the school yard where they are camped, towards the sun, silhouettes against light turned gold by wheat chaff dust. He takes off his cowboy hat and swirls it in the air to chase away the mosquitoes. Softly taking her hand, they amble slowly down the road as the sun sinks behind four conical grain bins squatting in a distant field.

On Sunday the crew loads into the van and drives 40 miles to a Mennonite church. They will not return until night fall.

"Farmers hate cattle, ranchers hate crops. I hate harvest and they hate branding. So I lease out my wheat land. Well, I do turn over my hay field."

Bill Reichelt is a rancher in a predominately wheat farming region but he is a very practical rancher.

"I also hate horses. When I had my first Jeep, I sent those horses to pasture to live out their lives. Horses eat hay and I'd rather sell hay than feed them. I replaced my '46 Jeep with a '52 Willys and now we use pickups."

Bill and his wife Doris own the Reichelt Cattle & Land Company in Carter. The ranch lies next to the Teton River and within whooping distance of the old Whoop-Up Trail. The trail was named for a Canadian Fort although the locals say the terrain was so rough whiskey barrels often sprung a leak and the freight drivers spent much of their time whooping it up.

The first Reichelts arrived in 1889 and the remnants of that ranch, a log house, still remain. Through the years various Reichelts added a windmill, a long wood shed, a Quonset hut, a trailer and – this really boggles the mind – a perfectly proportioned Victorian home, white as lace.

It is surrounded by a well-manicured green lawn that keeps the tawny bunch and buffalo grass at bay, a wrought iron Victorian metal fence, a bright flower and vegetable garden. It is magically out of whack with a ranch that at one point grazed cattle, sheep and horses over 25 miles of Plains and where teepee rings are plentiful on the many surrounding hills and bluffs.

Doris and Bill transported the house 60 miles from Great Falls where they bought it from the Anaconda Corporation. The couple are, of course, collectors. In the house is what you would expect – Victorian furniture, antique glass, porcelain eggs and a first rate collection of political posters and pins.

In the old shed Bill keeps a number of buffalo skulls he finds after spring run-off in the Teton River. Some display an elliptical hole chipped out in the forehead and Bill says Indian women made the hole to remove the buffalo brains.

On a hill overlooking the Victorian house a human skull was recently exposed after the snow washed away. Supposedly it was an Indian who died of smallpox and was buried at the turn of the century.

"If you are one of those environmentalists, we can stop talking right now and you get back home!"

The words are clipped, abrupt and staccato-fired by someone used to fast-handling a rifle at a running coyote. Glenda Reynolds is her name and she is surrounded by her four buffalo dogs. In the cab of her Scottsdale 4x4 is a .257 Roberts rifle and a .38 revolver in a scuffed up holster. She is baling hay three miles up a creek in the middle of 55,000 acres that comprise the 7W and 6X buffalo and cattle ranches. These ranches are in the back country of Garfield County, 21 miles of gravel and gumbo improved with eight inch ruts from Sand Springs and 57 miles from Jordan. God Help You on the last stretch that is more cliff than road. The postmaster at Brusett refers to this land as "For God's Sake Country."

Even though there are more antelope seen driving into the ranch than buffalo or cattle, the sign says, "Beware! Buffalo at Large."

Glenda's profile is honed by high cheekbones, a perfect nose, no-nonsense lips and a slightly stooped walk that makes you wince her-back-must-hurt-so-bad. Smoke-gray tinted glasses hide her eyes, snow-blinded when she was a child. Glenda, who has lived over a half century on ranches, manages this spread. Her father was born in a covered wagon, a collie baby-sat her and her mother used to ride with Glenda propped in a pillow on the front of her saddle.

"We're fighting a terrible battle. Those environmentalist shysters talk some wealthy widow into giving them money and they live well off it and attack us. They tell us how to run our ranches, how to rotate crops. They think this is a wasteland and people like you take photographs of a busted homestead but you don't show built-up ranches. I got buffalo and cattle here and you haven't seen nothing but lots of antelope, right?

"If we don't take care of our land, if we don't use our grass right, if we overstock or overgraze, we're cutting our own damned throat for next year we won't be able to use it. I only knew one rancher who overgrazed BLM (Bureau of Land Management) land and he was a greedy guy."

Glenda is just warming up.

"The environmentalists say they want BLM land cattle-free. They want the coyotes protected and the wolves brought back. They show a coyote in a trap in their city newspapers and say it is cruel.

"Why don't they show a coyote eating the hind end out of a cow and then eating the dead fetus and the cow is still alive? Why don't they show 15 dead lambs with just the kidneys eaten out by the coyotes?

"What with the high cost of machinery, of repairs, taxes, fertilizer, these people want to triple our grazing fees. It takes 10 to 20 acres to graze cattle in this country. We need lots of land. We feed the country and the people we feed want to stop us and kick us off our land."

Glenda is ranch manager for an Illinois owner; in four years she made the spread profitable.

In the fall Glenda stocks her groceries for the winter. She lives alone as her children are (a smile) grown and her husband is (a concentrated frown) gone. She takes care of the cattle herself, sews at night, reads and says that after working in minus 40 degree temperatures with three feet of snow on the ground, she goes to bed early.

I asked the usual question.

She smiled, more to herself than to me, and looked down at her dust-coated, paint-splattered jeans. Her cowboy hat covered her eyes.

"Yeah," she said softly, dragging on a cigarette. "I like it a lot."

"I have had six heart attacks. I am a ghost. I died once, for five minutes. Did I take a trip? Well, the bad things flew by, I didn't have time to get them all in before I came back. I lost my right eye from a stroke. Now I try to get in the movies for half price...I'm a tough old bugger. I was with Patton's Army and I have a Bronze Star to prove it. What good is it? My name? Call me Ivan the Terrible."

His wife Milly stands at his side. Ivan Zimmerman is partially paralyzed from his strokes but the glint in his eye is that of a mischievous kid. He has survived over 70 Christmases, making his way as a wheat farmer and cattle rancher. His dad came out from Iowa in 1919.

"My father was tired of shucking corn and he was opposed to gambling yet he became a wheat farmer, the worst gamble ever. Well, we got hailed out this year and three years ago there was so much hail damage our insurance put new roofs on the buildings."

What Ivan and Milly will be memorialized for is the Sod Buster Museum on Route 87 in Stanford. It is an eccentric yet valuable collection put together by them with no support save gifts from neighbors. They moved a pioneer cabin and a blacksmith shop to the museum site. They display a valuable collection of Indian clothes, photos of Charley Russell and Jack Dempsey and Tom Mix, a superb collection of hub caps from the Elmore, Flint and Hupmobile and other old cars, an Albino deer skin, kerosene lamps, old farm machinery, kitchen antiques, a pile of antlers, a mail wagon, Conestoga wagons, working outhouses and ephemera of all types that existed in Montana since the early homesteading days. They have Indian arrowheads and a beautiful collection of rocks from all over the world – Ivan was a lapidary. They also have a collection of fossils.

The Zimmermans live in what was once part of Benchland. The school, post office and everything but the gas station and community center were moved away. The problem was that the farms were too small.

"Lot of people went bankrupt at the time of Carter's embargo against Russia. We couldn't sell grain. Then some insurance company came in and bought farms as a tax right-off," says Milly. Many people left.

They miss their neighbors and their eyes light up when they remember them.

"I once slipped and hurt my back roofing," recalls Ivan, "and the next morning 18 neighbors showed up and finished the roof. That is the kind of people who lived here. Milly cooked a big roast and we had a ball!"

In 1996 Ivan sent me the following note:

Peter –
I lost my Milly to Cancer last August 4.
Enjoyed your photos. Have lost 74 pounds.
Poor Cook!...Ivan the Terrible!

North Dakota

If it were not for Catherine the Great and Tsar Alexander I, a century of circumstances would most probably have kept Brother Placid Gross' ancestors on the Volga and he would not be what he is now – a Benedictine Monk, farm manager of Assumption Abbey in Richardton and a man fiercely proud of his Russian-German ancestry.

In 1763 Catherine the Great wrote a manifesto, which she circulated among the peasants of southwest Germany. She offered free land, local self government, exemption from the military and taxes if they would develop the fertile steppes along the lower Volga. It was an eminently successful marketing plan, for 30,000 Germans started 100 agrarian colonies which eventually became the bread basket of Russia.

These early pioneers who took advantage of the offer lived in treeless steppes in houses of clay. Their fuel came from reeds, roots and grass. They were threatened by wolves and horse thieves and endured unbearably cold winters and boiling summers. From these hardships came the adage, "For the first generation – death. For the second generation – want. For the third generation – bread."

In 1804 Alexander I renewed the manifesto. He promised immigrants who farmed in the Ukraine and along the Volga 162 acres of Russian land and exemption from taxes and military conscription.

Someone in Washington must have been reading Russian history as the Homestead Act of 1862 promised settlers 160 acres of free land.

When the steamships became a trans-Atlantic flotilla and the Northern Pacific Railroad crossed America, their marketing departments penetrated Europe and used the lure of free American land to fill their ships and trains.

With the thousands of first farmers to the Plains came the ancestors of Brother Placid. The Russian-Germans from the Volga were short, stout people who, when they arrived on the Plains, wore long coats with sheepskin collars. These people preferred to sleep in a wagon than pay 10 cents to sleep on the floor. They had the experience to homestead in North Dakota; they were accustomed to the cold and to hard work, and considered the American plains as beautiful as the Volga steppes. Experienced wheat farmers, they brought the hard winter red wheat which is now planted across thousands of acres of the American "steppes."

"They toughed it out," said Brother Placid, who is tall and lean, "but now you also have to be intelligent to be a farmer."

Assumption Abbey was founded in 1903, four years after Richardton was established as a Catholic town on the Northern Pacific Railway line. The abbey had a seminary, prep school and a college, which are now closed. Today the monks raise cattle, operate a printing press, garden, produce honey and host seminars. Brother Placid oversees 400 steers and calves and is often found in the fields, baling alfalfa.

The monks don cassocks over their work clothes to pray. They end the day in the warm light of their lofty cathedral, singing a harmony so peaceful and reverent it makes one cry for the voids in life. The next morning, Labor Day, one of the psalms they sing ends this way:

Lord, give success to the work of our hands.
You turn man back to dust, saying, "Return, O children of men."
For a thousand years in your sight are as yesterday,
now that it is past, or as a watch of the night.
Lord give success to the work of our hands.

Merle Clark stands on his grazing land that overlooks the Little Missouri north of Marmarth. Across the river in the distance are capstone buttes and hills smudged with white bark and limber pine. The buttes are striated in streaks of dark brown, maroon, and red – a landscape once burned and heated by some great force. This gray river and the tans and red of clay and soil mark part of the Hell Creek region, an ancient outcrop of land 60 million years old.

A thin brown line about 2 ½ inches wide threads across some of these buttes. It is called the KT line, the signature of an ancient catastrophe that killed every dinosaur in the world; no dinosaur fossil is ever found above that line.

Merle's land, which feeds 250 head of cattle, borders one of the world's most fertile dinosaur fossil fields. Merle is an auctioneer, rancher and fossil hunter, who keeps a tyrannosaur femur in his garage, along with a reconditioned Model A. In fact, Merle and other neighbors are nationally-recognized dinosaur excavators. The museum they started, the Pioneer Trails Museum in nearby Bowman, and their dinosaur digs attract an international batch of paleontologists.

Merle drives down to Marmarth and onto a back road that snakes through flat fields of wheat abutted to a brutal landscape of scoria. Merle pointed to the bluff where the KT line threads horizontally half way below the capstone.

Merle and his neighbors have found in this region a complete t-rex, a taurosaurus, triceratops, and unidentified vegetation, fossils, fish, turtles and snails. His latest find is a "duck billed" dinosaur fossil, complete except for the head, which they hope to uncover.

"This was a subtropical flood plain," Merle explains. "Then the dinosaurs died within a 24- to 36-hour period. Charcoal is found near the bones and there must have been a helluva fire. Experts argue over what happened but I'm a creationist rather than a paleontologist. There was a lot of water and maybe a flood. You find the same marine fossils above the KT line but no dinosaurs. Crocodiles can exist in mud."

"This is the greatest t-rex area in the world. Of the 14 that have been found, half of them came from this area, from South Dakota to Montana, along the Hell Creek. I've found t-rex teeth marks in a triceratops fossil. T-rexes have a soft stomach and not a good breast plate and a triceratops could gore him bad. I think t-rex was a scavenger and they followed the triceratops herds, just like the wolf did with the buffalo."

Merle sifts an ant hill for bits of dinosaur bones. The ants have a habit of bringing fossil flakes to the surface.

"Years ago, a fossil hunter was out here, I believe in Montana, when an Indian band ran him down. They liked nothing better than to stake a man to an ant hill and slit open his legs. When they caught him, they searched his pack and found nothing but rocks. The Indians didn't trifle with people who they thought were mad, so they let him go. He had just found a new type of dinosaur fossil."

Not too long ago cattle rustlers worked this area until vigilantes stretched a few over near the Powder River. Now it is fossil rustling. The stakes are high; one complete dinosaur skeleton was sold to the Japanese for $360,000. The latest discovery is oil – lots of it – in the middle of the dino fields.

In July of 1992, Eric Sevareid, one of the great CBS commentators and writers, died. In his obituary in the New York Times was the following quote that only a Plains person would write:

"...Travels in all the continents have not lessened my love and respect for America but deepened both, in spite of the distressing spread of our vulgarities. There is civilization of the heart, too, and the goodness of Americans, the evangelical strain, has not disappeared..."

Sevareid was born in Velva, North Dakota, a land of wheat fields and sunflowers, tall-shouldered grain towers and minimalist Lutheran churches.

Eric was 13 when the bank, where his father worked as a cashier, folded. The Sevareid family moved to Minneapolis. Many people, who have moved frequently, appear to build their core values early in life. So it was with Eric.

Helen Blomquist Kramer was "the angel of blue and silver," as Eric wrote decades later. She sat in the school desk in front of him. He fell in love with her – and he loved her all his life.

Helen Kramer never left town. Her blond hair is now white but the blue eyes are bright. She lives across the street from where the school they attended was located; it was torn down years ago. She is a widow with a gracious manner and an acute memory of the days when she was Eric's schoolmate and sweetheart.

"Eric," as she calls him now but back in the early school days he was known as Bud or Buddy, "was a regular kid. He loved baseball. He loved fishing the Mouse River. We used to walk across the wooden foot bridge and cross the baseball diamond and there was a path down through the woods to the swimming hole. Our mother made us take an older woman with us. When we walked down the path we screamed, 'The Girls are Coming! The Girls are Coming!' so they would jump out and put their clothes on.

"I was the little girl from the first grade on who all the boys fought over. I never

let them carry my books. Eric always sent me a valentine but one year Ticky Tillapaugh sent me nine. When Eric visited in 1955 and we were talking in this room, he looked across the street and told me, 'I remember when I beat up Ticky Tillapaugh in the trees over there.'"

"Eric always kept in touch from the time he left in 1924. In 1930, when I had graduated, I told him I had a special boyfriend. I didn't hear from him until he came to town in 1933 and he found that I had married and had a three weeks old baby boy. He didn't stay long but after that he started to write again.

"Eric wrote about me in every book but one. I was always the golden-haired girl. In one of them he mentioned that when he was upset over something he would revert to the time when we were young and he could not...how did he say it?... 'stroke the golden hair of the girl who sat in front of me in school.'"

While Eric traveled within the history that shaped the 20th century, Helen remained in Velva raising a family. She turns and looks out the window.

"Eric called me in June of 1992 when he had cancer. He said he felt better. Then the cancer came back and he died a month later."

The room in which she talks soaks up silence. There is a gray rug on the floor and thick curtains are tied back from the windows. It is cool despite the heat of the midday. The room is not over-decorated nor cluttered with collectibles. Helen Blomquist Kramer sits neatly in an upholstered, delicate Queen Anne chair, her blue eyes focusing on a memory, a slight smile on her face. A grandfather's clock marks time. She recalled how much she wanted to stand with Eric in the prairies as he appeared in the CBS documentary on his life and the history he reported.

"He loved the prairies. I love the prairies. This is my country and this is a small town with simple living. I never wanted to live anyplace else...never had the chance, in fact. I don't regret it. I love this country."

"Is this town dying?" Paul Klindworth echoes my question in his small store stocked with canned goods, junk food and tobacco.

"No! It's already dead! They just haven't buried it yet!" His face reflects that period of life beyond old age, and he knows it.

A grain elevator that looms over the Soo Railroad tracks, a county road and a stand of cottonwoods screening a clump of houses barely identify Hamberg. It has the specter of a ghost town. The gas station, choked by rogue lilacs, is deserted. The price for super premium on the American Standard Gas Company's pump is 44.9 cents; the last sale was for 1.9 gallons. There is a large ball field where stands a small frame building with a sign nailed on it that says, **"Welcome, Hamberg Diamond Jubilee, July 5, 1986"**. The door is locked but the roof is caved in.

There are about 30 houses and 20 residents in Hamberg. Half of the houses are vacant. The town began dying when the quarter- and half-section farms were consolidated into two-, three- and four-section farms. The large schoolhouse, once handsome but now bleached and forsaken, closed in the 1950s when schools were consolidated. The older folk, when they retired, moved to nearby Harvey, into retirement facilities where, says Paul, some are living better than they ever have.

Paul's brother Clarence owns most of the houses in Hamberg, including the schoolhouse and the gas station. Paul owns three. A house and lot can go for $1,000, not including water.

One of Clarence's houses is a bereft, two-story structure isolated by a rim of cottonwoods and a large lawn turned to hay. It was once owned by a Norwegian immigrant.

"My grand-uncle Chris, he was a big man, about six-foot three, tough but good-hearted," says Gary Nelson. "He had a repair shop and did real well. When I was five, he was 72 and I remember sitting on his lap while he played whist with my father. That is a favorite game of the Norwegians.

"The next day his wife, Lilly, went to the store and when she came back she found him upstairs. He had hanged himself. The sheriff wouldn't go in the house so they called my father. He brought me down with him and we went upstairs and

he was hanging from a rafter. His eyes were open and his tongue was out so far.

"The family story is that when he was young man in Norway, he worked in the woods. One day he got drunk and killed a man, they say over a woman. At that time they hanged a man for murder so his family sent him to America.

"He had been planning his suicide for a while for he braided the rope very carefully. Norwegians, you know, they keep a lot inside them.

"This town," and he nods towards the main street while sipping whisky from a cup, "there're lots of stories. It used to be called Viking but the Germans must have gotten the upper hand because they wanted to name it Hamburg. The Norwegians fought back so they compromised and called it Hamberg."

Edna Pforr holds the highest salaried job in town as the Postmaster, a position she has held for over 15 years. She has seen the number of rented postal boxes slip from 40 to 20. Edna lives with one of her sons within walking distance of the post office and is proud of her vegetable garden. She is slim and has a wry but pleasant smile that, along with her kindness and sense of irony, has made her the mother to everyone in town.

"For 30 years my husband and I farmed. It was not a big farm – four quarters – but I liked it. We had tough luck on that farm from the day we first married. It would hail on our land and ruin the crops while the storm would by-pass our neighbors. We lost our wheat so we switched to milk cows and then there was a drought and we had to buy hay from Minnesota. There was a weed in the hay and the cows ate it and all of a sudden they lay down and died. We lost the herd.

"Then we had sheep and they got a fever and keeled over and died in the spring. This is the way our whole life was.

"Finally we sold out – you know, the big farm eats the small farm. So we moved to Hamberg. Three years later my husband had a heart attack."

Statistically, Slope County is on its death bed. The minuscule population echoes the falling economy. There are few people under 35. There is little construction and water and tax revenue, although the new oil boom may change that. So it comes as quite a shock to see so many happy people of all ages at the Slope County Fair, many of them arriving in new pickups pulling shiny horse trailers. They must not know they live amid statistic squalor.

Amidon, a handful of buildings centered around a court house, is the smallest county seat in America. The fair buildings and rodeo arena are pasted between the town and sloping fields of wheat. The fair is held in early September and is structured around 4-H kids showing their livestock.

The rodeo acts as the grand finale. The rodeo stock at the fair is scarred and mean and there is an ornery attitude shared between rodeo riders and their mounts. There is no flag carrying rodeo queen to commence the rodeo, instead the event begins with a fancy riding display by volunteers from nearby Dickinson who call themselves Custer's 7th Cavalry, Rough Rider Unit. The music and words that accompany their show wring tears of pride from the toughest buckaroo.

Most everyone at the fair wears a belt buckle won in a rodeo and many walk with a gimp. A cowboy's walking stick is sold here.

"Yeah," says a young rodeo rider, who so far has avoided injury. "It's a stick for old cowboys with bad legs so they can take a leak and not piss on their boots. It's got a flip-down trough."

A day before the rodeo some kids are roping and riding calves in the arena. A calf drags one on his stomach across the arena, another gets stomped on.

"Dammit!" he says, holding his head, and then ropes another calf.

No adults are around.

People here remain independent and resilient. They have made peace with time; they let it pass at its own pace and try not to harass it. These North Dakotans slow life enough so they come to know who they are – most already know where they will be buried.

Neighbors are scarce and often live closer to each other by horseback than road.

A cowboy explains that love holds these people together – a love for the land and for each other. Neighbor relationships are built on compassion and above all trust. "You have a lot of trust, you're going to have love," he says.

Dixie Davis and Chris Germann are best friends who live on ranches in Rhame. They belong to the Hoof and Handle 4-H Club. In this fair Dixie showed Scotty, a German Shepherd who won Grand Champion. Chris won awards with Annie, a cross-bred goat, and Chelsea, a Suffolk lamb.

"What are you going to do when you finish school?"

"Run a ranch!" they answered in chorus.

Mountain men gather at this fair to display their handmade crafts, compare their old and new black powder rifles and to have a shoot. George Summerfield, a gunsmith, and his son Pete are there. Pete just returned to live in North Dakota after eight years in Florida.

"My wife told me she didn't love me anymore, and she left with the kids," was his reason for returning home.

Pete was a teacher and correctional officer in Florida but more than anything he suffered burnout. He described the predicament he found in Florida.

"Both parents are away at work and the kids come home at 3:00 and have nothing to do but get in trouble; there is no one to help them with school or give them discipline. Families have no pride; I've seen parents switch a kid's shirt or trade kids with other families to double hit for welfare checks. I blame our society, which demands too much from our people to make money rather than make a home. The government wants us to spend and tell us what to do.

"You know what employers love in Florida? People from the Dakotas. They know we work and are responsible and do our best. We're always there in the morning, so they love to hire us. We know how to read and our parents gave us discipline.

"Why did I come back? Good hunting, fishing, open spaces and freedom."

The fair ends after the rodeo with a relaxed and happy affair at the beer hall. John and Corinne Getz drink Coors from paper cups, celebrating, in a happy and sad way, the end of another year.

They began to speak out about Slope County.

"It's open," says Corinne. "We're free. We do what we want to do."

"Way before government programs we were conserving the land to make it better," adds John. "Now they don't want us to drill oil wells and they want to protect

sparrows, which are nothing but a pest. Why do they come out to bother us? We don't go to Minnesota and tell them not to build a shopping center because it is on fertile land."

For 50 years the Getzs lived on their ranch and worked cattle and grew wheat.

Their happiest moments?

"Raising our five children," Corinne answers. "We had a good life and five children. They were good children and that was the best years of our life. I milked the cows, and raised kids, chickens, geese and pigs. We sold cream and eggs."

"When I worked out I got a silver dollar a day," says John. "We always worked with horses."

The Getzs left their ranch eight years ago; age and health was handicapping their ability to ranch.

"The saddest day of my life," says Corinne, "was the day we left our ranch." Then she hugged her husband and gives a cheerful, and sort of wistful, smile. Corinne died five months later.

Wyoming

Prior to 1974, before the town was built, there was nothing but windswept buffalo grass. Wright is now a compact community that owes its existence to the nearby coal strip mines. It is neat as any suburb with plots of green grass surrounding two story homes with RVs parked in the driveway. There is a hospital, a school, a health club and a mall, all in pristine condition. This town is circled, within the immensity of this country, like a wagon train.

Yet this comfortable community seems like a ghost town. Two people are in the mall. Another dumps garbage into a trash bin in front of the football rally pyre at the high school. There are two gravestones in the large graveyard. No cars are on the roads, nobody walks the sidewalks. One man is painting marks on curbs that need to be replaced. He wears disposable gloves so the paint does not contaminate his hands.

He says Wright was first a trailer park set up by ARCO and then grew into what it is today. Trains carry out the coal 24 hours a day, 365 days a year and there is enough of the resource to mine until 2017. A mine worker makes about $50,000 a year with overtime.

He suddenly stops talking and his face turns blank. He adjusts his hard hat, mumbles something about work and turns away.

"No Photographs Allowed" is written on a sign attached to the gate of the Black Thunder Mine near Wright. A guard is standing in front of the security building.

"I love it here," says the guard, who moved from Wisconsin. He extols the climate, the hunting, the snowmobiling, the fresh air and the friendliness. He is proud of the land reclamation the mine does and points to the fields across the road covered with buffalo grass and a couple of horses and antelope. Not long ago it was nothing but the leftovers of strip mining. He tells me antelope and even kit foxes wander through the security gate.

"May I take your photograph?"

"God No!" he says, aghast, and turns away. "I'd lose my job. Come back on Monday. They'll give you permission."

The mines use mammoth trucks to move the stripped coal. They are over 18 feet

tall and weigh 250 tons loaded. The tires are as tall as a goal post, and I want to make a portrait of a worker against one of those immense tires.

On Monday another Black Thunder security guard gives me a sour, smug smile attached to a "No." She says the office told her to say no photographs of anyone, or anything.

The Jakobs Ranch Mine is east of Wright, on the highway to South Dakota. They have mounted a sign more explicit than the one at Black Thunder.

It reads: **"No trespassing. All visitors and vehicles register with the guard. All vehicles entering or leaving the mine site are subject to search. Solicitation and distribution of literature by non-employees is strictly prohibited."**

Below it is another sign that warns of explosions and yelping sirens one minute before blasts.

From a distance Wright is hidden by folds in the land and the strip mines and derricks appear microscopic within the grassland's lonely immensity.

If a town is marked on a state map, it means it is alive – people are living there and there is a post office or at least a gas pump. This is not true with Clareton, which is on the map and as empty and debilitated as any true ghost town should be. There is a wreck of a dance hall, a stumble-down post office, the remains of a home and a one-room school house. The store, which once sold wind chargers and dishwashers, along with canned food, is no more than wood slabs and bits of iron strewn over the ground. The town was named for Clarence Townshend, who founded the post office that has been closed for about 50 years.

South of Clareton are rolling plains, a couple of trailers and a jack pump grave-yard. A couple of miles east of town is the Darlington Ranch. Eric and Lisa run the 3,700-acre spread and are the third generation of Darlingtons to ranch on land Eric calls desert.

Eric, who went to school in Clareton, says The Texas Cattle Trail, founded just after the Civil War, ran between their ranch and Clareton. Wagon tracks can still be spotted in sections. Cowboys drove cattle through until 1896.

The most memorable moment, Eric recounts, is what happened near Clareton in 1903. A fellow by the name of Diamond Slim, so named because he worked for the Diamond Bell Ranch, robbed and killed a homesteading couple, buried them and bedded sheep over their graves. Diamond Slim tried to sell the jewelry of the murdered wife, who was pregnant. He was finally arrested and locked up in Newcastle, where he confessed.

Neighbors of the murdered couple did not take kindly to Diamond Slim's grisly act, so one night they met at the stone corrals, built by horse thieves, and rode 30 miles into Newcastle. They snatched Diamond Slim from the jail, hauled him to a train trestle, looped a rope over his neck and heaved him over.

It is not the first time western hangmen misjudged the length of the rope; the one around Diamond Slim's neck was too long but not long enough to reach the ground. It yanked off his head.

The vigilantes rode back to where Clareton would grow and die. Along the way, one of them heaved the brass jail key into a stream.

The local undertaker sewed the head on backwards so Diamond Slim's toes pointed into the casket and his head pointed out. They displayed him like that for a week in front of a local store. Ladies and gentleman waited in long lines to have a peek.

The stone corral where the vigilantes first met remained for many years as a local landmark, until a rancher used the stones to build a foundation for a new home.

South Dakota

David and Janet Paul, Iowa farmers, moved to Faith in 1976. Their neighbors in Iowa wondered why they left, their neighbors in Faith wondered why they came.

"Our Iowa farm was near Omaha," says David. "and when the interstate came in, people in Omaha moved there. It was the type of town where we never locked up anything, but that changed quickly. One morning I found 50 gallons pumped out of my combine and then someone stole the hydraulic cylinders from my disk harrow. So I left. Besides, Iowa was plowing up every hayfield and pasture to plant corn and beans and there wasn't much left of the cattle business."

When David was a young man he worked for a cattle feeder near Pierre, South Dakota, and met a 90-year-old rancher with a 30,000 acre spread who told him, "Go on, Sonny, build your castle. This is the country to build it in." And that is what the Paul family did. They now ranch and farm 22,000 acres and how they succeeded is a primer on survival and growth.

First they leased land and Janet worked as a school teacher. When land dropped from $100 an acre to $40 they bought. Later they purchased another 80 acres which they considered insurance.

"We always bought land," says David. "We never carried health insurance until a couple of years ago, after we paid off our land. We never carried crop, liability or fire insurance. We didn't insure our house. We assumed a calculated risk."

"We had a daughter with a stomach blockage and a surgeon had to fly in," adds Janet.

"They knew we didn't have much," continues David, "and the cost was $200."

David bought used tractors for about $2,500, saving over $82,000 for a new one.

He grew alfalfa and ran cattle. He never bought a TV for his South Dakota ranch.

"I'm up at 5:00 in the morning and over the radio I get five minutes of world news and so far, when it comes on, it says the world is all still there. So that's good news. Then they give me the local weather and I'm off and running. Janet didn't like what was on TV so the kids read every Louis Lamour book and half the books in the school library and that didn't hurt them any."

To make a success of ranching in his part of the world, a family, according to David, needs to work about 6,000 acres.

"Oh, you can do it on 3,000 but your son will never ranch with you and it will be a starving outfit all your life."

"Agriculture out here cannot service 10% loan interest. A hired hand can never accumulate enough to lease a place, stock it and have the machinery to operate it. That only works under partnership deals or if he has a father with a ranch and they keep expanding. Lot of young people now, all they can count on is winning the lottery."

David and Janet, and their sons Roger, Daniel and John, work their property.

"Don't make it too easy for your children or they'll start going away for the weekends. They have to realize the responsibility of managing and running a business."

David drives to a high spot on the land where the sky is a blue dome over a horizon-bound land, burned brown from winter kill. He climbs down from his pickup and looks around. Fox holes are dug into the hillside.

"I like land. I like to stand on a piece of land and say, 'Land is my thing'. This to me is a sign of achievement. Success is to own your own land and not owe on it. Your land...yeah, it's kind of my place in the world right now."

Stubb Monnens is retired now, and raises pheasants, chukars and Canadian honkers near Buffalo. He was a sheepherder, possibly the world's shortest sheepherder, although it made not a whit of difference.

"I see the world from four feet up and the rest sees it from five feet down, that's the difference," he says.

Stubb custom-designed and built two sheepherder cabins for his short stature. In 1947, the Lemmon postmaster made a special saddle for him. At first he rode quarter horses, then, as he grew older, he switched to a Shetland and quarter horse mix and finally to a Shetland. Stubb has horsebacked over most of Harding County and he has never once let his size interfere with his work or his life.

Stubb's happiest moments were herding sheep. In 1946, he shepherded his first flock of 850 and he once oversaw 3,400. He did this for almost 30 years, up on the hills where the wind can be curt as a woman's slap and the high spots are marked by "stone johnnies" – cairns constructed by sheepherders.

"Best job I ever had. You see, the boss comes out and tells you to do this and that but after he goes you do things yourself the way you want to. You're your own boss.

"Biggest problems? Nothing. I never had a problem in my life. Well, maybe it was taking days off from herding, wondering where to go, what to do. The boss came out one summer and told me I had a couple of days off the next week. Well, for a week I sat there watching the flock and wondering who to visit. It's hard on a guy's mind thinking of that time and what to do and to take advantage of it. It got so bad I couldn't eat, sleep or do a damn thing. The boss came out, looked at me and said,

'God, you look like a skeleton!'
'Well, the next time you're gonna give me time off, don't tell me until the night before,' I replied."

Stubb remembers the names of all the border collies and horses he raised; they are a measure of his life. His worst experience occurred when he was roping a horse and it slipped the noose and caught Stubb by the leg. The horse dragged him over the rocks and cactus and burned holes in his shirts and rubbed the hide off his arms.

"Yeah, that was an interesting afternoon. Spent 21 days in the hospital. Lucky to be alive after that one."

He recalls the 40-hour stretch when coyotes killed 27 lambs, and how golden eagles and fox will kill sheep. But mostly Stubb recalls the beauty of living in a horse-drawn sheepherder's cabin, up on a hill with his flock, where the land stretches beyond the mind.

"People may think I'm nuts but there hasn't been anybody who enjoyed life more than I have. I never been east of the Mississippi and I don't care to go. I never been to the west coast and I don't care about that. I wouldn't live in a city if you gave me half of it. Probably city people would say I'm poor. I'd still be out there with the sheep but the days got longer and I couldn't get back on my horse."

Stubb sips coffee in his trailer while remembering these days, and for a moment forgets the present as he looks nowhere in particular, his eyes unfocused, a quiet smile on his face.

Lawrence Brown said his folks came to Buffalo looking for a good drink of water, so they homesteaded a quarter section that could sustain six cows. Now that land has expanded to 6,000 acres and is worked by Lawrence and the families of his two sons.

Lawrence writes a newsletter called *From the Deep Plains*. It can be sharp, witty, belligerent, irreverent and funny:

We as a people and this spot on the continent are in a minority. Our forefathers a couple or three short generations ago were solicited to come from Europe to settle and develop this last major frontier. America had supposedly freed the slaves, killed off most of the Indians, and herded the rest to a few reservations.

America's political mentality has always been a mixture of greed and thoughtlessness with a few pieces of compassion and do-goodism mixed in to make the whole thing confusing. Native Americans were systematically destroyed and conquered until they were a minority, physically and politically helpless. Then, rather then accept them as citizens into our culture, we set them apart on reservations. That way the problem could be perpetuated another few centuries.

Black folks were captured like animals and brought here to free the nation's founders from menial labor. Beyond that, they were bred and propagated like a developing livestock herd for more economic value. A combination of fear of the potential power of slaves mixed with a smidgen of human reason brought about the Civil War and supposed freedom.

Women, our feminine majority, were kept in submission for centuries until they exploded and threw enough rocks to get the vote three-quarters of a century ago and equality has now nearly leveled off....

The point of this history lesson is to get some focus on where we aggies and plains people are at present. It's somewhat akin to losing Russia as an active enemy. People need someone to fear or hate, especially our government does and without a whipping boy, we are adrift, our sense of purpose diminished.

But fear not, this new challenge is being met. Learned folks from the nation's universities, some politicians, part of the media, and a host of others whose bread comes from sources other than the sweat of their brows, have formed an informal allegiance. For lack of a better term, we may as well refer to it as the "Eastern Intellect."

What better sacrificial lamb could there be than the non-violent, non-militant tenders of the nation's pasture cows and related service people? People talk about some new Indians or whipping boys – it is us – three or four million village and rural people of the Deep Plains states – hovering between the 98th Meridian and the Continental Divide.

Since our rainfall is limited and the original homestead settlement couldn't stay here in permanent numbers, the Eastern Intellect reason that the rest of us should be sent to some kind of a reservation, annihilated, or at least moved. Not much different than the Indians a century or more ago. Do anything to put this Deep Plains land to a more philosophically loftier use. Ted Turner and Jane Fonda are pointing the way with tax scheme buffalo ranching in Montana, New Mexico and Nebraska.

This could be a new frontier of bureaucratic boondoggles. Billions of tax dollars, or grandchildren's debt, could be pumped into a dramatic new wilderness if we natives could be gotten to hell out of the way. Even the loftiest champions of conservatism and free enterprise could find tax shelters on the wreckage of our lives.

The winter wind is so strong that the snow can blow sideways for three days before it grabs on to the ground. Snowplows patrol to break through wind-compressed snowdrifts blocking otherwise bare roads. There is not much difference from being in the Plains or on the seas during a gale. On the Plains you may freeze to death and in the sea you may drown.

About a half mile from the fence, which was humming but not bending in the wind (face your car away from this wind, open the door and chances are the hinges will be so wind-wrenched the door will not close) is the town of Hoover.

The Hoover family founded the post office, a bank, creamery and the store, which was built in 1902. The property traded out of the family and in 1976 Jim and Leona McFarland bought it for a ranch headquarters.

"Hoover is on the map," said Leona, an attractive woman with a smooth face, blond hair and an aura of self confidence, "not because we have a post office, which we don't, but because we sell gas." The Hoovers run 300 calves and 500 ewes. The store is something they keep as a meeting place for neighbors; the bank and creamery have long since closed. The McFarlands are the only residents of Hoover.

Nebraska

Behind Burr Oak School, District 63, Custer County, is a tornado cellar. Sarah Jane Graham has never opened it in the five years she has taught there, for fear of rattlesnakes. A prairie dog village is only a couple hundred yards distant. Swings hang in the school yard along with a maze made of tractor tires. This one-room school is on a prominent nub of a sloping hill with a three directional view. The few trees along the creek below the school are just beginning to bud.

The grass is putty-colored, bleached by winter on this first day of spring. Two weeks ago children were sledding on the hill and now meadowlarks, the Nebraska state bird, are singing arpeggios as they perch on the barbed wire fence near the swing. Robins were seen today for the first time this year.

Inside is a piano which Mrs. Graham plays. There is a world globe, an American flag in the corner next to the blackboard, an Apple Mac IIC computer and a small library behind the dozen student desks. There are bathrooms for girls and boys and a microwave sits on the lunch table.

Mrs. Graham teaches nine children from kindergarten to the sixth grade. This school does not have what most parents demand – there is no lunch program, no school busing, no janitor, no assistant teacher, no cook and no superintendent, and what Mrs. Graham is paid would make a city teacher snarl.

Mrs. Graham believes in this system, as she is a graduate of a one room school-house, as well as the University of Nebraska, and has taught in Ethiopia.

"The state is anxious to close these small schools but we have a lot of local support. What is best about this system is that I have the same children year after year. I know where their weak points are and what to work on. In a bigger school the kids switch teachers every year and there is no continuity."

Mrs. Graham is a silver-haired, handsome woman with keen blue eyes and a quick smile. She dresses with style and carries herself proudly. Like most one-room school teachers there is a touch of steel in her sense of order and discipline.

"If I have an average child I expect them to do average work. If I have a very bright child, they have to do better than average work. I want them to be proud of

what they do because they have done a good job. I feel a one-room school produces students who are better prepared as they learn to work alone. They learn to be interested in learning."

Brandi and B.C., who moved to the region from California, go to the Burr Oak School. They were taught in classes of 30 students and had teachers who were more interested in having them play than learn.

"It was a struggle for them at first, for they weren't accustomed to doing what they were told," says Mrs. Graham. "Here they can't do just part of an assignment and hand it in and take a poor grade. They have to do it right, or do it over until it is right."

"When I was in California," says B.C., "they used to beat me up because I am small. Here they call me shrimp but I don't care."

"We were born in a little log house in Montana and then we went to California. We all wanted to get out and we came here. Dad's a cowboy. I like working on the ranch and I like animals. We have a bigger house and the water is good.

"When we got here and it snowed for the first time we were so excited my mother and all of us went out and played in it!"

family came up from San Antonio in 1912 to homestead. She runs the ranch with her daughter Rhonda and her husband Bill and the seasonal help of her all-women hay-stacking crew.

Sitting around her kitchen table, soaking sacks of coffee in cups of scalding water, she lets loose.

"A rancher finds in his sheep pen three grizzlies all set for breakfast. He scares three of them away only to find another is about to attack him. So he shoots it and the law takes him to court and fines him $4,000 for killing an endangered species. Don't we have a right to protect our livelihood or ourselves?

"The people from Lincoln and Omaha want to protect the wildlife and take our land. Why, you bring in a load of alfalfa and 30 deer ride in with it. We can't ditch and draw a meadow anymore because of those environmentalists. We can't build a road across our land without going to the government.

"These people want to take our country back to what it was before, but do you know what it was like then? The Indians used to burn the grass so the game would be driven to the river. When my family came here, this land was mostly sand and you could track a horse over it. We put in a lot of hard work through the years and when there's a good year of rain the grass is up to your stirrups.

"You don't own a ranch, it owns you, and there is constant work to keep it going, to pay the taxes and hope to break even. The taxes we pay per acre are greater than what we paid for land in the 1920s and 1930s. Only a damn fool is in agriculture."

Janet gives a gimlet look, as if someone might take up the challenge. She takes another puff on her cigarette and then stubs it out. On the wall over the sink is a framed motto:

May you have food and shelter
A soft pillow for your head
May you be many years in heaven
Before the devil knows you're dead

The stacking crew arrives and begins to prepare their tractors.
"Why all women?"
"They're easier on the equipment," she replies.

Follow the oil slick road north from Ashby, then, when it ends, take the first two ruts east over the Sand Hills for two miles. They lead to the Box K Ranch. Janet McPeak wears a baseball hat advertising a feedlot. She is a slender woman of small bones who walks slowly; a sharp intelligence burns in her gray-blue eyes. Her

Driving west on Route 92, under a brutally blue sky, are endless rolling hills of green grass combed by the wind – a golf course for giants. There are no McDonalds here, no Pizza Huts, no Gulf, 76 or Amoco gas stations, no souvenir shops, no Dunkin Donuts, no cops, no tourists, no motels and one telephone booth. Three cars pass on a 66-mile stretch. There are more cows and horses than people and houses. This is the Sand Hills.

On a bend in the road before Arthur a sign proclaims this town of 128 people is in the middle of God's Cow Country. An exclamation to that point are the fences that parallel the road into town – a gnarled, worn-down cowboy boot is stuck on each post. There must be over a hundred of them.

In the center of town is the culprit...Ed's Custom Boots and Dan's Boot Repair and Rose's Saddlery. Inside Dennie Rose is sculpting a saddle for Ed's Dad. He works on three at a time which takes him about five weeks; in the last 18 years he has made 200 saddles.

Dennie had a penchant for working leather ever since he was in grade school and made his first belt. He apprenticed to Wes Fuesner, a master saddle-maker who learned from his grandfather. Dennie then went to Texas State Tech to finish off his training.

Dennie's saddles are narrow, flat, wide, high or low in the front or rear, whatever the customer wants. He has his clients sit on a saddle in his shop so he can take measurements and then he sculpts the layers of leather to those measurements. He draws a tooling pattern and embosses the saddle. The tooling and amount of silver raise the price of a saddle but most sell for $1,200. He finishes every saddle with his signature – an embossed rose on the latigo keeper.

Dennie is so well-known that a French leather worker (cowboy clubs, where members dress and ride western, are popular in France) apprenticed under him.

Rose's Saddlery is much like a barbershop in that people congregate there and tell tales and myths of their region. There was a story about a rancher, disgruntled

with trespassing hunters, who mounted an automatic shotgun set on sync with the propeller of his Piper Cub, and took up strafing the trespassers. The conversation meandered to the tale of the headless body that was probably a game warden and the head was never found because, most likely, it was stuffed down a badger hole. There were other older stories of Texas gunmen hired to run off squatters, of a piano that traveled about and finally found a home in a whore house in Lust, Wyoming.

Dennie, pausing amid the storytelling, looked out the window and saw a man cycle by, his bicycle loaded with packs. His comment is typical for a Sand Hiller who rides only a horse and a pickup:

"You work your legs off to give your ass a ride."

On a sandy road in the Sand Hills of Garden County, Nebraska, leading to nowhere in particular:

Four dead cottonwoods, a couple of live green ash. A small barn 14 feet tall, once painted red, now weathered. Two front windows, blind, black holes. A windmill's shadow slices into a watering trough filled with fine, blown sand. Bunch grass, needle grass, corn flowers, blue bonnets. A small desert frog.

A large bug ponderously climbs an ant hill.

An eight by eight beam with four rusted coffee tin tops tacked on it. A round, ten foot corral post, silvered and half-buried in the sand. A shattered, ripped, shredded section of corrugated tin. A chicken coop. Coils of rusted barbed wire, a cow's bleached leg bone. Half of a brick.

Grasshoppers whir through wind-disturbed grass.

An outhouse once white, filled with porcupine droppings. The door, twisted off the hinges, shotgun blasted. A lean-to with floorboards 12 inches wide. Eight feet of wire dangling from a telephone pole. A rusted bucket, an iron hoop 10 inches in diameter, a stack of skinned tree limbs.

A piece of metal folded over on itself pokes out of the sand.

Animal and bird tracks scurried on a floor of wind-sifted sand. A refrigerator lying face-up. An antique kitchen cabinet, painted white. A broken spindle from a chair. Feed bins under the windows, opened for horses to stick their heads through. A coffee can, an empty bottle.

A swallow's nest lined with partridge feathers.

Evening, when the hill shades this skeleton of a ranch, three mule tail bucks trot down a cleft gully to feed on tall grass where once the front yard stretched. All are in velvet and one is a five pointer. A squall hurries through and from the gray-black sky drops a rainbow. Grass hills glow as if brushed with gold.

Clarence Spencer owned this ranch but quit it in the '50s and moved to Arizona. He died a couple of years ago. Barbara Hartman is cutting hay nearby with an aged John Deere tractor and she hopes to buy the abandoned ranch. She wears a red T-shirt and has a wide smile. In the winter she teaches school.

When Margaret Hawkins inherited the ranch from her husband Virgil, some thought Margaret would fail. Fail? This woman, who can fly an airplane, operate a back hoe, geld a stallion, bake an apple pie, ride professional rodeo in her spare time, and (when she was young) had herself branded, on the knee, *fail?*

Margaret Hawkins has fine blond hair cut short, a pug nose with a small indentation, lips that are neither sensual nor tough. Her index finger is whacked out of shape (by a horse) but otherwise her fingers are long and tapered to blunt ends.

Margaret does not look strong but she is as sinewy as beef jerky and tough enough to run successfully, with the help of her daughter and son, Virgilene and James, a 10,000 acre cow-calf operation outside Arthur.

Horses are Margaret's passion.

"I'll ride as long as I can crawl to the barn. I love horses. Some people ride naturally, some study it but we all have to work on it and that takes a lifetime. I got a horse whose biggest delight is putting cattle in their place. I just go around for the ride. We have good communication."

Margaret has 60 horses on her ranch. Most are quarter horses although she likes to mix hot blood with cold blood – thoroughbreds to quarter horses.

She and her daughter Virgilene spend part of the year following the professional rodeo circuit, a tradition Margaret started over 30 years ago. She has a combined horse-trailer and camper in which they travel to rodeos throughout the region. One of her barns is an indoor arena where she and her daughter practice barrel racing.

"From riding there is a good feeling between man, nature and God. As I get older and face some tragedies, I think about that. I get up every day and Bless the Lord and I can't think of living a better life. We have a special feeling for the land as we are at the mercy of the elements. Farmers and ranchers do things logically, not like business people.

"Sometimes, when we are moving cattle in the morning fog, the light breaks through onto the hills and the fog opens and we can see the clouds. It is on these beautiful mornings that the soul is restored. I have a love of the land, a love for a handful of dirt."

"I have a love for the land, a love for a handful of dirt."

"*W*hat'd you catch?"
"Bluegills!"
"How many you got?"
"Thirteen."
"What are you going to do with them?"
"Use them for bait for catfish.
Wanna see a snapping turtle?"

Mitch Meyer, Matt Lucas & Matt Meyer
at the state park, Arnold.

The Nations

Fred Dubray is on a mission to bring back the buffalo. He is a rancher who lives on a bluff overlooking the Missouri. To the west, as far as the eye can see, are rolling plains of buffalo grass that have never been plowed and belong to his nation. Here the herd of the Cheyenne River Reservation graze.

Fred is a Lakota, the tribal nation familiarly known as Sioux (a slang word adapted from the Chippewa which means serpent). He is also a former rodeo rider, a Vietnam veteran, and chief of the 33 member Tribal Buffalo Council.

"Black Elk prophesied that to get our people back together the Sacred Hoop must be mended and when it is, the buffalo will come back," says Fred.

"Our way of life was intertwined, the Lakota and the buffalo," continues Fred. He was sitting in his kitchen, finishing up dinner. Outside the wolf and coyote he keeps for company began their paen to night. "Buffalo provided our spirituality and it is why we say prayers when we kill a buffalo and thank him for providing for us. They give us food, clothing, utensils and shelter."

There are now 135,000 buffalo on the American continent, slightly more than the number of cattle slaughtered every day (In 1800, before the West was settled, there were 60 million buffalo. By 1900 less than 50 survived. Many white ranchers such as Ted Turner now raise buffalo and with the rebirth of the buffalo ranches a conflict has developed on buffalo husbandry.

"White buffalo ranchers vaccinate their buffalo, pull teeth, cut off the horns and fatten them in feedlot pens. It is a domestication process that takes away all the respect.

"A friend who was with me at a Denver stock show watched buffalo being led into the ring with their horns cut off and they huddled in a circle, scared, their tails down.

"'It reminds me,' said Willie, my friend, 'when they sent me to boarding school

and cut my hair off. I was ashamed to be an Indian. Look at those buffalo. They are ashamed too.'

"Some white ranchers who have an unruly bull will get rid of it for they want a docile herd or a young herd. That unruly bull is a survivor and is vital for the development of the herd. You don't kill him or cut his horns off. Wolves took the weak and sick bulls. Wolves were replaced by hunters who killed the strongest and biggest so what they shot weakened the herd. That is their policy – to replace wild animals with domesticated animals.

"Buffalo are wild animals who are survivors," continues Fred. "They do not need cultivated grains but can live on native grass, which, when it dries, retains its nutrition, which tame grass does not. In the winter, a buffalo will slide down a snow hill to brush the snow from the grass and then feed up the hill. When a blizzard comes up, cattle drift with the wind and pile up on a fence and may die. Buffalo face into the wind and weather the storm. Unlike cattle, they can put off calving until after a storm."

The tribal association has recently purchased a truck-mounted slaughter house from Sweden, where they are used to process reindeer. The truck can be driven into a field where the Lakota perform their ceremonies and then kill and process the selected buffalo. Fred states that such a method minimizes the release of hormones and adrenaline which taints the flesh when the animals are penned and slaughtered. He knows that range-fed buffalo is an organic meat.

Fred sees the return of the buffalo linked with the rekindling of the Lakota spirit.

Young Man Afraid of His Horses lives in the Medicine Root. He is a truant officer at the Little Wound High School in Kyle and is also a rancher, dancer and warrior. He is tall with wide shoulders tapering down to a lean waist; he moves with the grace of a cat. His face is rough-textured, but handsome. A small mustache covers his upper lip and there is a compulsion to see behind his dark glasses. For all his strength there is a gentleness – forged, perhaps, by a tough childhood, his early penchant for fights, his combat experience in Vietnam, and his battle with alcohol. The latter battle he conquered with the help of a vision quest and a medicine man.

Young Man was temporarily paralyzed from a fire-fight in Vietnam. When he was recovering, he had dreams of a person dancing but could never see who it was. One day the dancer became distinct, and Young Man realized it was himself.

Young Man is a tribal dancer. He dances at pow-wows throughout the west to help people. This man, in his words, uses his power to defuse power. He is a philosopher who hesitates in his thoughts, then expresses them in a rush with pure simplicity.

"When I dance I become another person. I am my father then, and I am an eagle. I dance to take bad feelings in and to give good feelings to my people. I dance to the drum, which is the heartbeat of the buffalo. When I sing my voice is the elk. Before I dance I smudge myself with sage. This gives me the power to dance and I paint myself so the spirits can see me.

"My dance is a prayer. I pray for all relations and friends, four-legged and two-legged and for all relations who have passed away. I ask them to help me in my prayer and dance. I holler to let them know. I dance for healing. I dance for the people. I pray to our God, who is the same for all of us. I never dance for money."

Young Man does not allow his photograph to be taken, so I asked if I could photograph his shadow. He ponders for a long moment.

"No. But you may take a picture of my dance costume. Then I am not me."

One of Young Man's sacred spots is a cliff edge at the end of a field that looks down on a gullied landscape of badlands. To the east is the trail Big Foot followed to Wounded Knee. Below is where some hid from the cavalry in the winter of 1891. Cedar trees run along the ridge. To the west are the sacred Black Hills. North is Bear Butte, also sacred. A tranquillity flows through this land and at dusk, the coyotes sing and the sky and cliffs blend into a blur of dark reds and smoky blues.

"I pray here," says Young Man, "because of the sound in the pines and because of the cedar, which is sacred. Here is mother earth, here is life. You call it badlands but it is not bad."

Young Man makes a tripod of pine branches and from that hangs his dance costume. The buffalo mask can only be used by people who are warriors and have had a vision.

"The buffalo gives me power and strength. So do the elk teeth hanging from it. The abalone is sacred and we use it in the Sun Dance. The ermine skin represents all the four-legged animals that live on the ground. The small medicine wheel on the horn is a gift and it has power. The blinds on the mask are so people do not know who I am, but also they keep me from seeing any bad.

"The eagle feather on my staff represents my family but the feathers on the dream-catcher are my immediate family. All dreams come true and we dream that our families will unite and help each other, for that is the only way we Lakota survive. We dream of ourselves as a large family and we need to help the children become part of that family.

"The horse hair is power that gives me strength to dance, as does the buffalo tail

on the bottom of the staff. Horses are powerful in our family. My name means that people in my family receive power and strength from horses," he concludes.

As the sun went down over the Black Hills Young Man spoke of his past and himself.

"I am a common man. I learned from my past to respect myself. You must respect yourself before you can respect other people; teachers must start here. We Lakota believe that all religions will be one and that all people are one. When we experience prejudice and hatred we must learn to shake hands with the person who offended us and walk away from that enemy. This is how we count coup. They who offend us will wonder about that handshake and then they will begin to learn.

"It is the Lakota way not to talk bad about people and not to be negative. We talk about the good things in people. There must be forgiveness for everybody."

When Young Man stops talking darkness dims the badlands and stars begin to pierce the night.

For most of this century the Lakota were smothered. Many young Lakota are learning the ancient ceremonies and traditions from their elders. The Sun Dance, the most sacred ritual of the Lakota religion, is coming back. Many Lakota are learning to speak and write their language.

"There is no culture without language," Young Man said. "For instance, the word for sun and woman is the same in our language. Without sun there is no life and without woman there is no life. They are related and the words in our language are related. Our culture is embedded in our language. That is why the government tried to take it away from us, and that is why we are bringing it back."

Lakota, according to Young Man, will be the only language used in Little Wound High School in Kyle by the year 2000. It will be the first reservation school to revert to its own language.

"I pray here because of the sound in the pines and because of the cedar, which is sacred. Here is mother earth, here is life. You call it badlands but it is not bad."

Many Lakota believe the elders scattered through the hills around the Medicine Root River are the caretakers of their culture. Medicine Root is not on the map; there it is called Kyle.

Francis White Lance is one of the young Medicine Root people who is learning to be a spiritual leader from these elders. He lives with his family on the outskirts of Kyle in a trailer. Next to the trailer is a meditation house made of hay bales. Next to that is his sweat lodge. He has shaped the sapling frame so that the ceiling traces the path of the stars. In 1995, he held his first Sun Dance.

To Francis, the Lakota are the caretakers of the earth and there is a revolution coming, not violent, but soulful. He is a social worker at Little Wound High School and he believes his job is to pass on the Lakota culture to the young.

Francis takes pride in his lineage. In a worn photograph he treasures the images of three brothers who survived Wounded Knee. On the left is Daniel White Lance, in the center is Joseph Horn Cloud and on the right is Dewey Beard. Daniel and Joseph survived 15 wounds received at Wounded Knee. The clipped feather on Daniel's pipe bag signifies a horse was killed from under him. The single eagle feather worn by Joseph Horn Cloud is the badge of a veteran warrior. This is what Francis wrote about his great grandfather and himself. The story of Daniel was passed down to Francis by his uncle, Johnson Last Horse.

Daniel White Lance killed many cavalry soldiers and still was able to walk out of Wounded Knee. Wounded six times, he crawled into a snow bank and a coyote came to talk to him. The coyote told him to be strong and that they would help...to keep the people alive. The coyote then licked his wounds and he was able to make it to the stronghold in the Badlands.

I have inherited the legacy of my grandfather along with my relatives and the Lakota people to carry on the Lakol Wicohan (The Lakota way of life). I have a bachelor's degree in western philosophy and a master's degree in theology. I have been studying why cultures and people can't get along.

Basic linear thinking is the problem. I found out that linear thinking began when Euclid wrote the first book on geometry. In linear, or axiomatic thinking, there can only be one right and one wrong.

Lakota thought has this idea but always holds it within the perspective of the circle. There can be many rights and wrongs depending on how you look at a situation.

The medicine wheel entails both linear and non-linear thought. This is the paradigm of paradigms. The medicine wheel is the Lakol Wicohan. It teaches you to walk in balance. If cultures and people could learn this, then there could be better relations between peoples in the world.

On a bluff at Wounded Knee, where two Hotchkiss guns fired into Chief Big Foot's people, is a rectangular gravesite protected by a fence. The remains of 146 Lakota are buried there, including children and women. They were killed two days before the end of 1890 by the 7th Cavalry. It was sheer panic followed by a massacre; accounts say women were shot in the head and back, some while protecting their children. Twenty soldiers were killed that frigid morning and 16 later died of their wounds. A corporal who manned one of the Hotchkiss guns received the Medal of Honor. It was the end of the Indian Wars and the beginning, for the Lakota, of what they call 400 years of sorrow.

Offerings of tobacco, fruit, corn and flowers hang on the fence of the mass grave. Outside the fence are more recent gravestones of Lakota. Some died in the World Wars. One grave marks the remains of Buddy Lamont, who was killed in 1973 by a sniper when the U.S. Government put a halt to the American Indian Movement at Pine Ridge.

Amid gravestones to the north of the mass grave are four thin tree limbs pounded into the ground. Tied on the limbs are narrow strips of colored cloth, flailed by the wind. The flags represent the four directions: yellow is for the east, black for the south, red for the west and white for the north. The colors also represent the four colors of the earth's people, *"All My Relatives"* as the Lakota say.

A lone person, Little Eagle, is selling dream-catchers. He made them in two sizes from bent pieces of wood with gut stretched inside, like a snowshoe. Feathers and beads are attached to the interior strings.

"They catch bad dreams," Little Eagle says.

A fall wind chills the hill and the land has turned brittle waiting for the first snow. There would be few tourists until spring.

Jewish survivors of the Holocaust and Vietnam veterans have suffered post traumatic stress syndrome – they feel guilt for being alive. Jean Hammond, a child development specialist at Pine Ridge, believes the Indians suffer the same affliction. Post traumatic stress, child and sexual abuse, alcoholism and alcohol fetal syndrome have become the collective burden of her people, Jean says, since the end of the Indian Wars at Wounded Knee.

Jean is a Lakota, born on the Pine Ridge Reservation who moved to San Francisco and made stained glass windows. She knew no Native Americans and had no "sense of Indianess." Through family ties and self-awareness, however, she "recovered her roots" and moved back to Pine Ridge where she earned a degree in child development. Her main satisfaction, she says, is giving a sense of worth to children and to help them overcome the trauma that has afflicted their parents.

Jean had a grandmother named Victoria, born in 1867 during the Andrew Johnson Administration and who died 100 years later during the Lyndon Johnson Administration. Victoria related to Jean the great nomadic circle her tribe made. They would leave their home in the Black Hills and travel to Kansas and Oklahoma and then back home. It was a circumference three years in length as they followed the buffalo.

The medicine wheel is so ingrained in the Indian philosophy that Jean took what she learned from her grandmother, from her college studies and from her Indian culture and from friends and forged her own therapeutic circle.

"We Lakotas talk in terms of harmony and balance in our lives. After Wounded Knee they destroyed our spirit houses, and then our spirit bag and our Sun Dances, so they destroyed our spiritual life. My grandfather, Luther Standing Bear, sang his death song when they sent him to school and assigned him a new name and cut off his hair. Catholics and Protestants split up the reservations and made sure we had no ceremonies. Our parents saw the reservation as nothing but a place of tragedy.

"Wounded Knee will not leave us, there is fear and our culture calls for 400 years of grieving," she comments in her office at the Pine Ridge hospital.

"Trust has been lost, it is in a bag and we have to take it out of the bag and bring it back, to be reawakened, as my father used to say. We are not born to suffer so much. Our ceremonies are coming back and I am thankful for the beauty around me. We must stand up and know where we are. This is *Inya*."

Jean's way of teaching her children to become aware is to describe a circle split into four quadrants. The first quadrant represents a person physically and Jean stresses the care of health. The second quadrant is the mind. The allies to an active and growing mind are teachers, families and extended families, which are so vital to the Lakota. The third quadrant is feeling, and there the therapist or a relative is an ally. Jean says this is learned by sharing and re-identifying culture in the home and school. The fourth quadrant is the individual. There people identify their own persona – "Why I am the way I am."

"I have children whose little bodies have been hurt, who have a feeling of tears and low esteem," she explains. "Sometimes I ask my young kids, 'Where are you?' and they say they are in my office. I ask them again and they say 'I am in my shoes.' And finally, they realize with a big smile that 'I am me' and they point to within themselves."

Jean is working on her own circle. She avoids trends and has stopped smoking after 40 years. Her ally is her grandmother Victoria, to whom she prays. Victoria was in the tent where Crazy Horse was brought after he was killed. She wrote 13 pages recounting those days, and included a description of Crazy Horse. It is written in Lakota.

"I made a promise to myself that I am going to learn it line by line and translate what she wrote," Jean affirms. "I am going to learn Lakota so that I can read it, write it and speak it."

Narcisse Heart is tall for a Lakota – a Yankton Sioux he calls himself – and because of his height or because of his coordination, he has been a basketball player for most of his life. He began playing when he was six, went to college on a basketball scholarship and played until a twisted ankle forced him to drop out. Later he played with a black team from Kansas City and was offered a position on a black team in New York City, but he turned it down.

Narcisse is now over 43. During the day he works as a custodian at Little Wound School in Kyle and hopes to coach the girl's team ("Everyone knows they are not very good and they need help," he confides.) He draws and paints, a talent he inherited from his father. Narcisse and his wife Cindy, and their two children live near Potato Creek in a trailer surrounded by blond buffalo grass and sloping hills.

To the side of the trailer is a basketball hoop mounted on thick posts. When Narcisse stands under the hoop holding his youngest son, T.J., he looks over seven feet tall. It is an illusion, however. He lowered the hoop as an ego booster for his eldest son, Jessie.

Colorado

Weld County is one of the nation's wealthiest agri-counties – it is home to factory-sized turkey farms and pig and cattle feedlot pens that are some of the world's largest. So it comes as a surprise that one of the most efficient operations with the least amount of cost is a 20-acre plot of vegetables known as the Monroe Organic Farm. It is run by two generations of the Monroe family in the small town of LaSalle.

At one time it was a 127-acre dairy and vegetable farm with one of the first milking parlors in Colorado. In 1957, Jerry Senior sold the herd, when he lost his hired hand, and then sold most of the land, keeping just enough to grow vegetables for his livelihood.

Jerry farms the way he was brought up to – pulling weeds by hand and using natural fertilizer. He saw no reason to change his ways in the 1950s when chemical fertilizers were aggressively marketed. Now the farm has operated over 50 years producing vegetables from land never stained with chemical fertilizers.

"It's not that we were organic-minded, we never did hear the word *organic,*" says the elder Jerry, a man with acute marketing sense. "All farms were organic. We just never switched. Now you bet we're organic-minded."

In 1993, the Monroes joined the Community Supported Agriculture program, an international group of organic vegetable farms that sell their produce to members. The Monroes figure they could produce vegetables and fruit for 1,000 families although they do not intend to go over 500. They now have 90 members who pay a fee to join and then pay for shares depending upon their needs. Some work several hours a week in the garden to lower their costs.

The Monroes plant 150 varieties of vegetables, flowers, herbs and fruit on their 20 acres. Sometimes the strawberry, melon or tomato crop is so bountiful members pick, at no charge, baskets-full to take home and can.

Jackie, wife and partner to the younger Jerry, still drives to farmers' markets in nearby cities with produce and also delivers vegetables to members. She writes a newsletter and creates recipes and instructs members on preparation and processing. Jerry Junior tends the fields and has expanded the operation with a root cellar, a solar dehydrator and a movable chicken coop. They shift the "chick-mobile," as they call it, to different fields so that the chickens can feed on insects, particularly potato bugs. Members also helped Jerry construct a greenhouse.

Jerry Senior talks about the advantages of their small farm amid such large operations. He speaks under large Chinese elms, planted in 1915 when the land was all sage brush save for a few trees along the South Platte river.

"Some of my neighbors spend $8,000 an acre to run their farms. Combines and tractors are expensive and so is interest. It's possible for a vegetable farm to make more out of a quarter of acre than a farmer does from 80 acres."

Because of the high cost, some of the nearby farmers have sold out.

"When they sell," says Jerry, "the mineral rights are often already sold and then the water rights are sold to someone else. A city person buys the house and a farmer buys the field and the equipment is auctioned. This is wrong, for there's no integrity left in this land."

Under one of the elms are over a dozen bushels of ripe, red tomatoes, freshly picked.

"Water is the big problem. We only get 12 to 15 inches of water a year. When we irrigate, we only take a quarter to a half foot of water from the ditch while a large farm may take water 24 hours-a-day for two or three weeks. Water is going to become the big investment here and that will lead to more bickering and litigation."

"When they sell, the mineral rights are often already sold and then the water rights are sold to someone else. A city person buys the house and a farmer buys the field and the equipment is auctioned. This is wrong, for there's no integrity left in this land."

About 30 miles northwest of Sand Creek, where, in 1864, Colonel Chivington and his volunteers massacred Black Kettle's Indian tribe, is the town of Wild Horse. Not much to say about the town – the first building went up in the early 1900s and all but one building burned down in 1917. It came back a little better.

Leona Schrimp has seen the ups and downs of Wild Horse. She was a lucky baby, for her birth in 1917 kept her father from going to war. She grew up in a ten-by-twelve-foot house on a quarter section of land, just small enough to break up with a one horse plow but not big enough to survive on.

"We saved a little and Dad increased the acreage," recalled Leona, "then that big red dust cloud came in from Oklahoma. We had no money in the thirties but we had chickens and always enough beef. We helped each other out."

Those who remained slowly prospered on cattle, and then, in the 1940s, on wheat. Their farms grew with tractor improvement.

"First Dad worked with horses and came home for lunch and, during hot spells, rested in the house for two hours. Then came the tractors. They were hot and the iron seats were hard but we got tractor umbrellas – wow, that was really cool! Next came tractor cabs and easy seats and after that we had air conditioners and radios. The tractors got bigger and so did the farms.

"Big cattle companies came in and four or five small ranches were put together to make one. Oil was also on this land. Lot of these people borrowed from the government and got subsidies. When the government pays for something such as land improvement, you then lose local responsibility as no one will do anything for the government. There are now a heck of a lot of millionaire ranches but all we got left are about ten families.

"Small ranches improved the country. We had kids in school and good churches and we grew up at Sunday picnics and on the baseball field. We knew everyone. Did government practices ruin the small farms? No, it didn't ruin them. It eradicated them!

"The best years of our life?"

We are sitting in her cluttered but neat living room. Leona's hair is a pure white, neatly made up. She does not move around well. She looks up and smiles radiantly. Her teeth are as white as her hair.

"The thirties. We were young and we thought all the men were so handsome. We always dressed well even though we were poor. We had ice skating parties on our ponds – the ice was so hard and smooth. We went fishing and enjoyed harvest get-togethers and round-ups. Once we made a trip to see Amelia Earhart's airplane. We had a sense of belonging as we had no money. We were a group of happy friends!"

In 1938, Leona married her friend Curtis who went into the cattle hauling business. They never left town and are one of five families who make up the 13 residents of Wild Horse.

Leona showed me a photograph taken on the Fourth of July 1936, of her, her soon-to-be husband and eight of her friends.

"Ed, Bob and Pat, they died recently. Ordean and Dorothy are dead. Verg was a patrolman, and he was shot dead."

She looks up from the album in her lap.

"I'm sort of worn out now. They'll be no nursing home for me. I'll stay here and be buried in the cemetery with my little boy. He's up there by himself all the time...my first child, born in 1949...he didn't make it through. I was 32..."

"God up there," and Joe points straight up, his out-of-whack nose and eyes raised, "is with me. Some people say I am magic. God helps me and some-times...yes...it is magic. I am always honest but not always perfect. Find the per-fect person, I say, and get on your knees and kiss his feet, for that is Jesus."

I met Joe Gaona at the Monroe Organic Farm in LaSalle. Joe is a mechanic and has a garage a few miles away in Eaton and trades mechanic work for vegetables – a lot of vegetables – Joe and his wife Rita have 11 children.

Joe, with his burliness, his black hair and smiling eyes was a brazero born in Minnesota and raised in Mexico; his family did contract farm labor from Texas to Minnesota. He eventually settled in Colorado where he met his wife Rita and, with hard work, opened a garage. A gifted mechanic, he knew how to put a car togeth-er but did not understand how it worked. He went to school and received an auto-motive degree, so the magic he practices comes from the classroom.

"I search for perfection. If I hire a mechanic, I tell him before I hire him that if I find a loose bolt, or something done wrong, he's out of here."

Supporting 11 children and putting a roof over their heads is a burden most peo-ple would leave on the roadside. Several times the Gaonas were forced to move because rental laws and town codes prohibited so many people living together. The amount of milk consumed at breakfast is gallons and the cost of clothes and sneak-ers cuts deep into the budget. Yet, Joe accepts all this with zest and good will.

"I do not have enough education," he tells me in his garage, where he is repair-ing my car. "I make sure my kids do their homework. One of my children rebuilt a car engine when he was 11, but they do their homework before they help me. My wife thinks I am too hard on them but I teach them to survive. They work for their clothes. Joey, at nine, was hired by an electrician to crawl into tight places. Adolfo at 14 drives a big tractor and cultivates corn and beets. I teach them the right things. I don't want them on the street, in gangs."

"Have your children experienced prejudice?" I asked. Joe stiffened before he answered.

"I don't want my children to say, 'I can't do this because I am not white, I am Mexican.' I tell them to always go for it and never say you can't do it. It's easy to use prejudice as an excuse."

Joe's garage is alone in a field three miles from town, on land owned by a friend, who has graciously let him build his business.

"I like it out here in the country. I'm free. No people are telling me what to do. There are no restrictions from the town and no bosses."

I had parked my camper between the garage and a cornfield; the shock my car needed would arrive in the morning. Under a tree is a tractor Joe fixed up and will truck to his father in Mexico. He sends his mother and father $50 a month.

In the evening, Rita drove out with four of their children who are sleeping overnight in the back of Joe's Dodge Ram. She brings fresh tortillas wrapped around pork and rice and seasoned with her salsa filled with a hot, clean fire. Rita sells it for $10 a quart. After dinner, I and the children sprawl in the back of the Ram and watch a movie on a 13-inch TV. Outside this cozy, little living room, the sky over the Rockies turns red and then blue as the first stars blink and the big dip-per falls into place. An evening wind rustles the corn stalks and carries the distant bawling of cattle. The children are soon asleep.

Joe has my Jeep in good shape by mid-morning and I drive off with two quarts of Rita's homemade salsa stashed in the Airstream.

"**I**'m a golf ranger."

"What's that?"

"I make sure everyone plays cool and moves right along."

It is 7:30 a.m. and there is no one on the course except this golf ranger, whose name is Bill Luff. He is hiding under a straw cowboy hat and has a growled, gravelly voice.

"Don't have much to do this morning, huh?" I then point to the green, which is why I stopped and give Bill a quizzical look.

"Why that's a green."

"Looks brown to me."

"We don't have much rain here and there is no way we could have real greens. The fairways, they're all buffalo grass cropped close. The greens are made of river bottom sand. We sift out the pebbles that are too big and mix in oil. Then we spread it around the cup."

An oiled green takes special skill and care, Bill explains. When the balls land on the green, each player measures the distance the ball is from the cup. Then they take a custom-made rake with prongs on one side and a flat bar on the other. First they rake a path from the cup to the edge of the green and then they smooth it flat with a roller. Everyone takes their shot along the rolled path, at the distance their ball landed on the green from the tee. When they finish, they rake the green in circles, smoothing out all traces of the path and their footsteps. They use different rigs for smoothing the green. The heavy roller is for the farmer kids to pull. The lighter one is for men like Bill, who is retired and moved from Denver to live near his daughter. He bought and sold bars.

"Any good bars down here?" I ask.

"Nooo. Only the VFW and two other bars. Quite a few churches, though."

"Town doing good?" (The town is Springfield, so deep in the southeastern Plains that the state tourist map covers it with a photo of pines and lakes found in the mountains.)

"A good crop of milo is coming up. Like any town in the boondocks, people are running businesses they don't know anything about, but if they are making a living, the heck with that."

The Springfield Golf Course has nine holes and the 70 or so members pay $25 a year dues and three bucks a round. On one side of the course is a field with feeding cattle. An electric fence guards the cattle.

"One guy hit out-of-bounds so he steps over the fence and got hit by the wire between his legs. Man, did he drop!"

In another direction is a junkyard. In a house adjacent to the course lives the town banker and his wife, who is custodian of the club's two outhouses. About a dozen women are members.

Rabbits, lizards, ground squirrels and rattlesnakes sometimes share the course with the players. The rattlesnakes live in a gully in the center of the course. Sometimes players lose balls down there; they roll right into a hole and Plains people do not ever stick their hands down holes.

"Watch out for dogies. They're real dangerous and they're a lot of them," said the driver of a road grader he was giving a rest in the ghost town of Keota. "What are dogies?" I ask.

"Rattlesnakes shedding their skins. They're blind and strike blind."

The Pawnee Buttes, just north of Keota, are miniature badlands. They are deserted on this late fall afternoon except for a golden eagle sailing in circles, his wings gilded by the sun just touching the horizon. Minutes later the sun is sucked under and the sky deconstructs into yellow and orange-red hues blotted with puff clouds the color of slate. The cap rock cliffs glow pink and then sink into gray as the sky cloaks itself in a rich, mysterious blue. The coyotes yip a greeting to the darkness which creeps in from the east and, like a slow paralysis, snuffs out the light. Then the stars and the half moon light up and sprinkle beauty into the night.

The next morning one of Keota's three residents is gardening by her house, a pail in hand. Sunglasses hide her eyes. She was tired by the summer hordes of tourists.

"People come here and say, 'How can you live in a place like this?' What right do they have to tell us how to live? We have our gardens and our animals and our beautiful views."

Her name is Betty Bevins.

"We're bothered by a lot of people here with no respect for the land or the property. They take things. Got that way ever since the publicity."

"What publicity?" I asked.

"This is the center of that Centennial book by Michener. They say he lived here but that is not true. He got a lot of information from a woman who lived in Greeley."

She mentions that Keota is in Weld County and in the southern part of the county are huge feedlot pens.

"It stinks down there...," she says, "stinks of money."

Keota became an incorporated town just before World War I. Betty was the last bookkeeper; she un-incorporated Keota a couple of years ago.

Betty's husband is the second resident of Keota. The third, who lives in a small trailer behind the state garage, is building a boat in which he plans to live after he

hauls it to California. Betty says she rarely sees him.

I mentioned that some city people would like to replace rural people here with deer, antelope and buffalo.

"Well," she answers, "we had a murder in this town once and if someone came to do that, it wouldn't hurt to have another."

"Who was the first?" I ask.

"Guy got axed. He wasn't liked and they stuffed him down a well, but not the town's well."

"How did they find him?"

"He began to stink. Three guys went to jail but not for long. They were pardoned."

The driver of the grader was about to trim one of the roads that seem to stretch from Keota to eternity. He explains he must keep the roads maintained for summer visitors and how in the winter he knocks down snowdrifts.

"Tourists," he spits. He is a heavy man, blunt spoken, with white hair. "So many tourists come here now I can hardly take a pee anymore."

"*I think what I remember more about this country is the first impression I ever had. When we came here in 1914 we came in a covered wagon. And they had more rain than they ever had before or since. It was completely covered with wild flowers. Gladiolus, but we called them niggerheads and then wild honeysuckle. Oh, there were all kinds of flowers, it was just like that as far as you could see. There was houses but mostly little dugouts or small houses and a small patch of farmland around them. Twenty acres would have been a big patch for anybody to have lived on. And there was no fences, it was just completely open prairie just as far as you could see.*

"And I remember that wind. I used to love that wind. But you see, there was no dirt because it was all prairie, grass. The wind could blow but there was no dirt and us kids used to like to run in the wind and we would hunt buffalo horns and arrowheads. I remember I had long hair. I don't know why they would do it but my brothers would make me unbraid my hair. They would coax me to. Then I would run and I was supposed to be a sail ship and that was the sail. The hair was the sail. Then they would try to catch me. My two brothers were younger and I could outrun them and they would holler about the sail boat. And we'd play for hours that way...

"They broke up the country for wheat in the 1920s. Eastern farmers, suitcase farmers, ploughed up the sod. Instead of prairie fires we had dirt storms. With a prairie fire it would come back prettier next spring than it was before. That dust bowl, it ruined farming completely. Dirt blew from '32 to '39 or '40."

...Marian Green, from her interview in the book by Jeff and Jessica Pearson, *No Time But Place, a Prairie Pastoral* (©1980 McGraw Hill and San Francisco Book Company. Reproduced with permission of The McGraw Hill Companies). The Green family homesteaded in the Colorado Plains near Campo.

Kansas

High noon on Main Street, Sun City. The wind is dead and the sun beats down hard; shade is a gift from porches. A brick building across the street stands lonely. Next to it is a bar and restaurant. The town is deathly quiet, like a dried up water hole. No cars pass. No lawnmowers whine. East, down Main Street, and west, there are no people, just two parked cars.

Ward's store is sparse, with a counter facing rows of shelves with few canned goods. A sewing machine sits on a table in the back and there is a coffee urn. Two men are seated in front of the half-empty shelves. They look me over as I enter.

"Come on and sit down," one says.

It does not take long to find out Ivan and Bill are retired, the population of Sun City is under 100, most residents work at the sheetrock factory in Medicine Lodge, not much happens in town, and people rarely drive through. Alma and Buster Hathaway ran the bar and restaurant across the street but she died a couple of years ago; now her widower Buster works alone. Actually, one family owns most of the scant town, and the post office building.

"It's not worth a darn," said Helen Axtell, Bill's wife.

The meter man comes in and reads what he has to read. A truck driver stops and asks about the condition of a back road. A state cop parks in front and Ivan and Bill perk up. The cop decided to drive the back way home, and buys a bottle of pop.

I ask if the town was ever feisty.

"Well, no, I don't think anyone ever was killed here," says Ivan.

"Guy did get shot in a bedroom. Shot in the ass," adds Bill. "Well, he was caught in the wrong bedroom."

I walk across the street to buy a beer. An evaporative air conditioner known as a swamp cooler makes a low hum. Cowboy pictures hang over the empty booths and along the opposite wall is a long bar, where Buster sits alone, reading a newspaper and sipping a beer. There is an old canteen hanging on the wall and stamped on it are the words "7th Cavalry." Two stuffed bobcats and a jackalope make up the decoration. I order a Coors and Buster delivers it in a frosted, very thick, glass schooner that looks like a wine glass. I admire it.

"One woman came in here and offered me $10 for one," recalls Buster. "I said no. She kept going up in price and then said her last offer was $200. 'Lady, I don't need your money. I need them glasses. They're not for sale.'" Buster shakes his head.

A kid walks in and buys a dozen Bazooka bubble gum. He leaves his bike leaning by the door. The swamp cooler keeps humming and the beer is so refreshing I have another, and Buster says it is on the house. He tells me about a buck with six points to a side killed with a muzzleloader last fall.

When I walk out, Main Street is just as brutalized by the sun, just as quiet as when I arrived. I see no one, hear no noise, see no cars, feel no wind. I walk quiet to the other side of the street, sit in the shade of the porch, and for a while, stop existing.

There is a softness to Emancipation day in Nicodemus, the oldest black community west of the Mississippi. In the evening, coolness seeps up from the grass and a refreshing breath of air sifts through the town. The next day the sun burns hot by mid-morning but a soft breeze rustles the Chinese elms and locusts in the park. A sense of tranquillity glides through this town.

What is it about this old community, founded by freed slaves – Exodusters they called them – in 1877?

It is their 116th celebration and 450 kin and friends have gathered with residents for this 1994 celebration. There is an easiness in their smiles and eyes. Maybe it is the blessing of the River Solomon that flows through this land, dipping into small stands of trees – a river refreshing and cold after a rain, nurturing corn and sun flowers and fields of wheat.

These days Nicodemus is home for older folks. Except for a few farmers, most of the young have gone to urban areas to make their living. Yet those who stayed behind – mothers and grandmothers, great-grandmothers, fathers and grandfathers – have more than a touch of iron in their character and a sense of family and discipline.

Rosa Stokes, mother and grandmother, born in Nicodemus and determined to die there, talks about the qualities she holds essential as she sits in the cramped living room of her house on a dusty road behind the town's center. There is a television in the room with a screen smaller than the bible pages marked with ribbons lying on the floor. Scores of photographs of relatives and friends are pinned to the wall.

"My daddy said he would always watch out for us and he did, he and Momma always had a home and food for us. They lived together 63 years before they parted in death. They didn't drink. They didn't smoke. They didn't whore-hop. When we needed them, they were at home. I worked the plow before I left for Denver and took up catering. At 60, I took a nursing test and passed higher than many of the young students liked. And then I came back and I'm visited often by my kin.

"The young come here and don't know an egg comes from a chicken, a ham comes from a pig and milk comes from a cow. They think animals are too pretty to kill. Well, I showed them. I used to kill chickens by wringing their necks while swinging them around. They just don't know about such things.

"Kids now, they have a liquor store and marijuana and television and parents are too busy to mind them. They come here and I make them do chores and they get mad. If you see someone who isn't yet five needs a spanking, they say, 'I'm going to call 911.' If they do that, the law comes out and puts you in jail and makes the children suffer.

"The trouble is people now listen man to man and not to God. People make money and think they become successful by themselves. They cuss rain and lightning and worry about wheat growing. Kids say they're not cutting the grass at the parsonage because they're not getting paid. What good is money when you don't know how to use it and haven't been taught the value of it?

"God told Adam about the apple. Did he tell Eve? No. There is no communica-

tion and there still isn't. That ugly face there, that TV, it brings out lies. You can't believe everything you hear on the news and the lawyers are crooked, the judges are crooked, for they take sides. Oh, yeah, I can talk. Everyone is out for the dollar. There is law but there is no justice."

The doors and windows of this small frame house are wide open, a habit Rosa begins the last week of March.

"I used to tell Poppa I needed fresh air and I didn't like closed doors.

'Stay out of trouble,' was his answer, 'and you'll never be locked in.'"

Rosa stops talking and glances out the open door, lifts her head and the room draws silent.

"In the morning, I look out, you know, across the way and it is so quiet and so pretty. It's that way in the winter. Anytime it is so pretty. Even on hot days. You look out and see the waves of heat and it looks like the ocean out there. But we don't have the wild sunflowers anymore that grew seven, eight feet tall. Now we have just little ones and there are new weeds with purple blossoms."

Rosa has a couple of rules for parents and children and she ticks them off just before dinner. The first is to teach children to listen and to do that, the parents must listen to their children. The second is to make a home. Children in homes help one another and do chores. There's a big difference between a home and a house. Third is that children nowadays want to be young adults, because they are bored. Their parents have neglected to teach them. The fourth is that children will respect other people and things if their parents also show respect. The fifth is that parents must have commitment and rules and teach them to their children. The sixth is that you need faith to exist, to live and to love. The seventh is to be nice, to thank people when they help you and to help them when they need it.

"Well," Rosa folds her hands and looks at me closely through her thick glasses. "I'm old fashioned. Just like an old fence," and then she leans forward.

"You look good. You're healthy and traveling. No one is traveling with you. In the morning when you get up you know it hasn't been just sunshine and nice weather but if that is the design in your life, of what you want to do, to be a journalist or a writer, it will work, it will work. And every time you get up and look out the door you can feel your body move, and hear, smell, see and talk. Think of these things."

Master Sergeant Williams is waiting for the parade to wind through Nicodemus.

"Might just as well relax...I feel good today...got a good night's sleep...I feel good now."

He speaks as if he exists beyond the strictures of time. There is the whisper of silence, he pulls out a pack of Lucky Strikes and lights up.

Nobody knows better how to wait than an old soldier. There are six here in their blue uniforms, cavalry hats and yellow bandannas – the last of the Buffalo Soldiers. Organized as black cavalry units in 1866 to serve in the Indian Wars, they were disbanded in 1944.

"They took our horses away for they was no match for the Panzers," says Sergeant Williams, referring to the feared German tanks.

For 23 years, from 1867 to 1890, the 9th and 10th Cavalry fought the Plains wars from the Rio Grande to the Dakotas. They used broken down horses discarded by the white cavalry and saddles that were remnants from the Civil War, and, at first, old weapons.

They lived in the worst quarters, were fed rations that were sometimes wormy, treated despicably by other soldiers and civilians and withstood the roughest field conditions possible. Against all that they had the lowest desertion rate in the Army, very little drunkenness, and became the most decorated units in the military with more regimental citations and Medal of Honors from the Indian to the Spanish American War. While they received hardly any public recognition, they did win a few other accolades. The Cheyenne named these troops Buffalo Soldiers. The term was one of respect, a result of their first skirmish.

"Segregation is a terrible thing, but the best thing that ever happened from segregation are the Buffalo Soldiers," says Sergeant Jones, who served with the 10th until it was disbanded in World War II.

Sergeant Williams experienced racism when he enlisted at West Point in 1939.

"It didn't take me long to learn I was a flunky. I had to get up early and clean the horses, clean the stables, take the horseshit out."

He transferred to Fort Riley and became a machine-gunner. When the 10th Cavalry was disbanded he was sent to Africa and France, first in an engineer battalion and then as a truck driver. He was discharged after the war but went back into the Army during the Korean conflict and, as a tank commander with the 758/64 Heavy Tank Battalion, survived eight campaigns.

"I was blessed. I've been shot at, strafed, bombed, mortared and grenaded. I had people next to me die, but I never got a scratch. The Good Lord was on my side.

"I never had any trouble in the Army. My people knew I wouldn't put them in any danger that I wouldn't take. Only trouble I had was with other master sergeants. I'm proud of my time in the uniform."

Sergeant Williams drags on his Lucky, holds it between his thumb and forefinger in the military way, so you leave hardly any butt.

"I look back on my eighth-grade education and, yeah, I did pretty well...pretty well."

The most admired and hated woman in the western world, during this century's first decade, was Carry Nation, sometimes known as The Hatchet Lady or Cyclone Carry. The legend began in June of 1899, at her home in Medicine Lodge, with a vision. In this vision she heard the words, "Go to Kiowa and I'll stand by you." And with that phrase her hand was thrown down in a chopping motion. The next day she harnessed her horse, Prince, to her buggy and, with rocks hidden in rolled newspapers, she set off for Kiowa. She broke up three saloons, smashing bottles of booze. They let her go, with a warning not to come back. Next she formed a branch of the Woman's Christian Temperance Union in Medicine Lodge. The new members and their leader marched on the local drug store and splintered barrels of whiskey. Her story was picked up in the newspapers, where they called her The Hatchet Lady. So she bought one, and used it to chop up bars in Wichita and Enterprise. In Topeka she learned what the inside of a jail looked like.

She was attacked so often by the pro-liquor faction she carried hat pins for weapons. Her fame traveled the world as she became the leading crusader against the drunken path and her lectures led the way for Prohibition. More than anything she was a Christian woman who, when meeting people, said, "Do you Love Jesus?"

Carry was married to an alcoholic and when he died he left her with a bunch of bar bills and a child who was "afflicted."

Fern Heublein's life has been intertwined with Carry's. She also lives in Medicine Lodge and her parents lived for a while in the Nation home. She is a devout woman and knows the effects of alcohol. She, like Carry, is a member of the Woman's Christian Temperance Union.

"I guess you could say Carry was part of my family," Fern says as she leads me through the Carry A. Nation Home and Museum that is filled with photographs and memorabilia of Carry Nation's ten years of radicalism. Fern walks with a tall, stern carriage and has an intelligence she directs with blue eyes that are more fair than compassionate.

"Carry had to go clear to the right to turn around the terrible things that were being caused by alcoholism. She was a fanatic in order to right a wrong."

Fern, like Carry, has had alcoholism in her family and for years Fern dressed up as Carry Nation and traveled and lectured about this crusader and what she stood for.

Fern likes to clasp her hands when she talks and her words come out as if already edited, not with anger but in a direct way.

"Our nation was founded on religious freedom," she tells me as we sit in her cool living room, her husband stretched out in a chair, recuperating from an operation. They are retired farmers.

"All our federal buildings have inscriptions on them saying *In God We Trust*. Our nation was founded on that but now we put our trust in the military and a President who is going to lead us we don't know where. We have faith in man rather than God and our values have slipped away. I think Christians are going to have to be crusaders, like Carry Nation, to turn this country around."

I tell her that I am not keen on the fundamentalists and she says she understands that but she feels sorry for the young people because they are not given proper values. She recited an instance in Medicine Lodge where there was trouble in the school between whites and blacks.

"I'm a strong believer in God and Christ as the head of the Church and if people really believe in God and give their own lives to His principals, then we will have good citizens."

"I never did see a photo of Carry smiling," recalls Fern, "but she was a master of public relations. I smile too much."

When Fern stood in front of Carry Nation's painting, dressed as Carry Nation and posed as Carry Nation, she did not smile.

New Mexico

The Spanish explorer Coronado, in his quest for gold, led the first white people to what is now Tucumcari. It took another 400 years for the town to claim its four decades of fame as a rest stop on The Mother Road, Route 66. In 1923, only a scattering of cars, trucks and wagons passed through the town. In 1926, Route 66 was strung from Chicago to Santa Monica, a distance of 2,448 miles, and the traffic count increased by thousands. That was nothing compared to what was coming.

Lillian Redman first saw New Mexico in 1916 from the back of a covered wagon when her family migrated from Texas and filed a claim at Santa Rosa. They moved to Tucumcari in 1922 and she has never left.

Lillian first worked as a "Harvey Girl" at the Harvey House restaurant at the railroad center. Eventually she became well-known for operating a Route 66 icon – The Blue Swallow Motel – given to her in 1958 as an engagement present from her fiancé. She has spent three quarters of a century watching people pass through the slight rise in the land Tucumcari is built on.

"The first group came through during the Dust Bowl. It was just a rutted dirt road and a long stretch from Amarillo...104 miles. The people were dusty, they were exhausted, worn out, filthy and hungry. They came in wagons, in Model A's and model T's and I never saw so much red beans and stale bread in my life.

"Almost all had children and that is what was so pitiful. The Salvation Army and the Red Cross ran bread lines. We put sheets over the doors and windows and wet them, to keep the dust out. It was rolled in black clouds and the wind blew awful hard.

"We shouldn't call those people Okies, they were everybody with a dream. California had movies, style, wealth and great promise. So when they were kicked off their land, lost and not knowing what to do, they went to where the promises were – California.

"Tucumcari was just three or four blocks – a couple of churches, some dance halls with ladies of the evening and a big camping area. We had a boardwalk and the railroad. These dust bowlers would stop here and often they didn't have enough money and would take some farm work before moving on. We didn't have much to offer. They were afraid of the Indians and the Mexicans who would steal from them. Bootleggers would also prey on them. Often they would travel in groups of six or eight wagons together. They were a latter-day pioneer group."

Lillian recalls all this sitting in a stuffed easy chair in the office of the Blue Swallow. There is a fireplace with a light behind the logs, a 1950s cigarette dispenser, a potted plant and behind the counter, a collection of stuffed cats and teddy bears. She sells one-cent balloons, sunflower seeds, lollipops, Life Buoy soap, postcards of her and the motel. A bible sits on a round table.

"The next group that came through, in the '40s, were the soldiers. We had trooptrains during the war, but after came the veterans. They were a different kind of people. They didn't have homes but their family life was conservative and organized. I imagine this was due to their training in the military. They had a better life as the Depression had eased up, but they were short of lots of things. They were searching for someplace where they could be happy, so they wandered and drove back and forth across the country.

"They had more to deal with than the ordinary person for they were putting

behind them their war memories. Even though some were married they couldn't share what was in their hearts. It was something inside of them; they were moody and at other times hilariously happy. I could tell by the mood they were in what part of the war they were reliving.

"We had sewing rooms and made garments for them. We repaired their clothes and made quilts. They were not settled and often the only clothes they owned were on their back."

The Blue Swallow is stuccoed coral and blue with 20 rooms and attached garages. A single room is as small as a monk's cell and mounted on the walls are old Carrier air-conditioners that wheeze and whisper the air around. A bathroom with a small shower stall, a wall-mounted sink and john takes up little space. The bed has a wood headboard and probably was ordered from a Sears catalog. The walls are blue and cream. A single rooms costs $11.13, including tax.

"After them came the hippies," continues Lillian. "They wouldn't work. They drank and took drugs. Their moral standards were low. They didn't respect marriage like a person should but went for free love. Groups would come through and sometimes they would get in trouble with local people. If a hippie saw a woman they wanted, it didn't make any difference whether she wanted them or not, they took her. They had no place to go and nothing to do when they got there. They were forever looking for the rainbow and I don't think they found it.

"They were the worst I ever saw, for they didn't respect people. This was in the early 1960s. They were going to San Francisco. They had a colony out there."

"They were the last group. By the 1970s we had kind of settled down to being human beings again."

In 1981, Interstate 40 bypassed Tucumcari and three years later Route 66 was decommissioned. Sections are as buried as the Santa Fe trail, parts of it are history, and some remnants are small strips that run through towns such as Tucumcari.

"You know, when you drive an interstate you want to see how fast you can go. You don't talk to anybody for there is just that road unwinding. Here you can see what our life is like. Europeans are traveling here to see how we live and many Americans are now taking a look at ourselves. I think people are slowing down. I think they are starting to look around."

It is early evening, the room is quiet. Lillian is almost all talked out and only two others are registered at the motel. A kerosene lamp stands alone on a shelf, as if hoping for an emergency. Before she says goodnight, Lillian explains the symbol of the Blue Swallow.

"The blue is for truth and the swallow is for happiness. Mr. Redman and I, that is what we had, true happiness."

Lillian has a card she gives to guests at the Blue Swallow. It is one she wrote.

"Greetings, Traveler," it reads. *"May this room and the motel be your 'second' home. May those you love be near you in thoughts and dreams. Even though we may not get to know you, we hope you will be as comfortable and happy as if you were in your own house. We are all travelers. From 'birth 'til death' we travel between eternities. May these days be pleasant for you, profitable for society, helpful for those you meet, and a joy to those who know and love you best."*

"We're a fourth-class post office but we're allowed a phone. Know why? Snakes. Rattlesnakes like to sun on the steps. One bull snake got inside and swished into the vault. Got a new linoleum floor then," says Nancy Felton, postmaster of Mills, town population of four. She is not one of them; she drives to work from Roy.

Mills looks like it barely survived a mortar barrage. The railroad stopped running and the tracks were torn up. Buildings were torn down or hoisted off their foundations and moved away. Others died of old age.

"It's a bad year for rattlesnakes," said Bob Dennis, who with his wife Peggy own the post office building (where she was post master for 31 years), the vacant lots next to it, and a ranch of about three and a half square miles. They live on a hill overlooking the post office. Bob is pouring cement for some steps. An open bible lies on a table by the chair on the front porch and chaps, spurs and a holstered revolver hang on the back porch. A dog not used to strangers acts as a doorbell. Poppa and Granny, as they are known, make up 50% of the population and have lived there for three quarters of a century. The Lucases are the other town residents, recently retired from Santa Fe.

"I came here when I was four, in 1913," Bob says. "It was a big town. The three hotels were always full, there was a flour mill where my father worked, grain elevators, a lumber yard, theater, a two-story hospital and three doctors. Wilson's Store was out of New York and they sold everything from sewing machines to threshers. They had pneumatic tubes to send money and orders between the floors."

"Don't forget the two saloons," Peggy adds. "And the churches."

"Why the population must have been about 700," Bill continues, "and the granary could be seen for miles around. The '20s were our best years and everyone was growing beans and grain on 320-acre homesteads.

"In 1915 this was the Wild West. There was no law. Guys rode up and down Main Street shooting at everything. There was killing going on and stealing wives. A woman rode out of town once and her horse came back and she was never seen again. It was pretty rough. Mother ran a boarding house.

"We went to school in a dugout about a mile from town. One day at noon we heard the darndest shooting and we looked out and saw this outlaw by the name of Higgins. He was on his horse, chasing Hunchback Hurtado and shooting at him. Hunchback ran to the schoolhouse and the teacher let him in and she barred the door. She grabbed and stuck him between two homemade desks that two of us sat at and pulled them over him. Old Higgins hammered on the door with his six-shooter.

"'What do you want?' asked the school teacher. Her name was Faye Evans.

"'I'm going to kill that dirty son of a bitch who ran in there!'

"Higgins was really drunk and just wanted to kill him, I guess."

"'You're mistaken,' said Miss Evans. 'He ran over the hill.'

"She kept that little man hidden and had us scramble out the window and stay at Wilson's, the big store. She let that little old man out at midnight and I'm sure he was running for his life and we never saw him again. George Higgins was the ringleader of a gang who lived in the Canyon. They made whiskey down there and used to rob the stagecoach from Santa Fe when it crossed the river."

"Tell about the time the rattlesnake made you burn your socks," Peggy says.

Gene Case lives just outside of the town and is the rural route carrier for the Mills post office. He is paid $13,000 a year to deliver mail six times a week to 22

ranches on a 58-mile route. He drives the route in an air-conditioned Ford pick-up with automatic windows and air conditioning. This land, once so rich in wheat and grain and beans, is now bleached by drought. Gene is also a rancher and runs about 50 head. He mentioned how one rancher received 40/100th of an inch of rain during the last rainfall while his neighbor Gilbert got an inch that turned his fields green. Rain, land and neighbors are reality and when other locations in the country are talked about, they exist as disembodied works of fiction.

"It was good farming here and you could grow anything and the town grew with it," Gene says as he drives the mail route, a contrail of dust streaming behind his pick-up. "We had the Southern Pacific railroad and a lot more snow and rainfall. Then the dust came in and brought darkness.

"Cows sold for $12, a calf for $2 and a hog went for 50 cents. There was no feed, and land went for $2 to $5 an acre but there were few buyers. Farmers couldn't get help. The land dried and they headed west in wagons. One came to my granddad and offered his deed for a dozen chickens, only my Dad didn't have any chickens.

"The government took back the land and turned it into the Kiowa Grasslands. Then they rented it to those who stayed, who switched to cattle and eventually did okay. I'm glad my family stayed."

Gene points to the lone trees that sparsely dot this land and mark old homesteads long since disappeared. Boards bleached like old bones pattern the ground near empty foundations and scattered about are pieces of metal and leather, dirt turned to dust and cowpies. A dry and hot wind whips the landscape. Gene says he wouldn't give 15 cents an acre for the land now, but one good rain would make it rich and wonderful.

Kyle Bell and Harry Daniel are day-work cowboys. They are freelancers, who are paid by the day or the job. Kyle is in his mid-thirties and lives on the New Mexico-Colorado border in the town of Kim. Harry is in his mid-sixties and resides in Des Moines, New Mexico. They had spent the day working for Casey Thompson, who ranches 25 miles south of Capulin. They checked cattle for brisket (a high altitude disease), for those who had eaten locoweed, and strays. After work, they drove Harry's old horse trailer to Capulin, and as they sorted out their gear, began to talk about cow punching.

Harry: "Oh, there's been quite a bit of change but not as much as where I'm working. We done it at the Spool Ranch same as we did 30 years ago. Just don't work as many men as we used to."

Kyle: "There's a lot more cattle and a lot less cowboys."

Harry: "We got more roads and more horse trailers so we can move 30 miles or more. Couldn't do that 30 years ago. Some are working cattle with four-wheelers."

Kyle: "I'd like to see them have a four-wheeler rope a calf. I was raised in Texas and worked on some pretty good-sized ranches. I worked up to manager. Then the ranch goes broke and I'd start all over."

Harry: "Or sell out. That's what happened to me. I run that Spool outfit since 1960 and the old rancher dies and the young ones sold out."

Kyle: "We northwestern cowboys are a little more colorful and stick to tradition. Texas cowboys wear baseball caps and tennis shoes and spend all their time in the cafe drinking coffee and saying what a hand they are. I'm a Texan so I can say that. I like handmade boots and saddles and I know how to braid rawhide. Lot of cowboy skills have been lost in places like Texas because they made things to be practical, such as big fancy working shoes and hydraulic squeeze chutes and electric branding irons. They done away with dragging cattle to the branding fire. I'm just enough of a romantic to keep the old ways alive."

Harry: "You get these new ways and, like me, I'm lost. I'm still trying to do stuff like I did 35 years ago."

Kyle: "Cowboys will last as long as McDonald's. In this part of the country you

need a horse to take care of those cows until they get to the feedlot. Long as some-one can ride a horse there'll be a need for someone to break them, but there will be fewer of them as we become more mechanized."

Harry: "You can't change oil now with a bucket. You got to take it to a dump someplace. None give me hell yet, but we're feeling the results."

Kyle: "Anything that anybody is doing to harm the environment is wrong and if you are doing something you ought not to be doing, don't do it.

"Four hundred years ago the Spaniards came in here. They converted those Indians they could and killed the rest or pushed them out of the country. They brought horses and cattle and sheep and goats and started to overgraze the coun-try.

"Then the Anglos came in. First they whupped all the Indians and killed all the buffalo and brought in hundreds of thousands heads of cattle and grazed the coun-try down to the ground and that's why west Texas is covered with mesquite. There was no conservation back then. It was the American Dream to get as much as you could as quick as you could before somebody else got it away from you. It's the American way of thinking that civilized the American West. We also ruined it. People who lived here didn't have to go to Wal-Mart. They could live off the land. They could drink out of every stream and every lake. They could hunt afoot and have meat all year round. People who lived back then took care of the place they lived in."

Harry: "We need to re-evaluate things but the environmentalists have gone over-board on a lot of things, like they want cattle off the BLM and then they say cow-shit is ruining the ozone."

Kyle: "It's too much asphalt and too many houses. Land should be set aside for wildlife. Why is it okay for us to live here and not okay for wolves? I don't think we have the God-given right to come in and wipe everybody or everything out that doesn't agree with our way of living. I think they should bring back the buffalo. They're better eating than cows anyway."

Harry: "Ranchers hate buffalo."

Kyle: "I'm not saying we have to give the land back to the buffalo and Native Americans. It's too late for that. I would like to see a place where the wildlife can live and it ain't for hiking, camping, for hunting or taking pictures."

Harry: "Nobody can take a picture or look at them? What good is it going to do?"

Kyle: "Not do us any good. Do the animals good."

Harry: "Well, first thing you know, you got so many animals in there they are all going to die."

Kyle: "Well, we can sell hunts."

Harry: "Yeah, but not take pictures? I chase coyotes all winter. I sure don't want all the coyotes killed off but they go killing calves, they get mange and scabies, but hell, I like to listen to them bark. I like the tune. I like seeing them out there."

Kyle: "I hate to see people or animals suffer for the benefit of someone else. There was 60 million buffalo on the Texas panhandle. Well, we got rid of them."

Harry: "It would be great to have cattle and a little herd of buffalo, but you can't turn the whole country back to buffalo like old Ted Turner and that Jane did by buying that ranch in New Mexico for buffalo. You can't treat buffalo like cattle."

Kyle: "You know what I like? I like keeping up the tradition and doing it proud-ly. I like being a cowpuncher."

Harry: "I like to go to the dances."

Outcast clouds rode north and storms hid out around the distant and worn out volcanoes – bumps on the horizon. Cattle flecked this land, sewn together by a highway and railroad track that lead into the center of Clayton.

Clayton is best known for the hanging of Black Jack Ketchum, a nasty, no-good train robber. People from Amarillo rode excursion trains to witness the festivities, which turned gruesome when a too-long rope pulled off Black Jack's head.

Across from the Hotel Ekland, where gunfight killings were once a popular pastime, is Isaacs True Value Hardware. Robert W. Isaacs bought the Clayton Hotel in 1900 and moved the hardware into it. In 1910 he changed the name from *ferroteria* to his own. Eighteen years later he asked his son to run the store.

"As soon as I was working, he quit," said Bob Isaacs, who was known in Clayton as Young Bob.

Over the years Young Bob built up the store and kept such eclectic stock that one cowboy said they have things in there older than Moses. The store carries sucker pipes for windmills, Victor coyote traps and wagon parts. In the basement, next to the dynamite storeroom which is no longer used, rope snakes up through a hole and can be measured in 40 foot lengths by markers painted on the floor. There are all types of large and small springs, kerosene lamps and just about anything a rancher might need – including modern appliances. There's more storage than selling space in this store and an elevator carries supplies up from the cellar and down from the balcony.

Bob's wife Bess works in the store, as well as his sons Mack and Dick. Bob is semi-retired; he gets up at 6:00 a.m. instead of 5:30 a.m. and only puts in 12 hour days.

"My sons all have degrees. I'm the least educated in the family. They tell me what to do. I'm a flunky."

"The town's been good to me. I like the business and the people, and they like me. We've lost population. The big ranches have taken over the small farms and there's not enough jobs for the young. This is happening all over the nation. What it means is that sooner or later we will grow again as people will need a place to live. This country will have a rebirth.

"There's crime in the big cities because there are too many people. We have better ethics here only because everyone knows everyone else. That slows you down some.

"No one likes to work too hard, you and me included. Thing is to have a job you enjoy, then it's not work. But some...they just don't have what it takes to get out and to be independent."

The Isaacs immigrated from Europe through Ellis Island, moved to Cincinnati and then came to New Mexico.

"This country for the most part is tolerant of everybody. There is a lot of prejudice, but it's in pockets. Jewish people came here after the Spanish Inquisition. They converted to Catholicism to save their hides and kept their Jewishness buried for years. Only recently they started to come out. We were always Jewish."

Bob leaned back in his chair. His office appears to be crammed with almost a century of the store's bills of sales. There is probably a receipt for the rope used to hang Black Jack in 1902.

"Do you know that a prominent Jew put all his money in the Revolution? Fellow called Morris. He was one of the financiers of the Revolution and he died broke.

"You know...," Bob smiled gently. He looked like a wise old owl peering through his glasses, "someone had to dig up the money."

Six months after I interviewed Bob, he died of cancer. His son David, an ace with the computer, joined his mother and two brothers to run the store and the odds are the name Isaacs will hang over this Clayton store for another century.

A branch of the Santa Fe trail leads through Capulin, just east of where a child was killed by a rattlesnake and where a frame house sits on skids in the middle of a field with a shallow depression in the center.

The story is that Don Morrow, who owns the land, concocted the idea that the field should become a lake with a marina on it. All those Texans and Oklahomans driving through on Route 64 to the Sangre de Cristo mountains would be sure to stop.

Don needed a store for the marina so he paid $1,000 to the railroad for the house and moved it twice before it landed in the middle of this field. Some say it cost him $3,000 in moving fees.

Then Don moved out of state and the idea dried up (so to speak) but the house remains. Tim Morrow keeps his cattle on the land and the most water this marina will ever see is sprinkled on it by a pivot irrigator.

Oklahoma

Bud Davis was 77 in the summer of 1994, when he spoke in the kitchen of his shaded and cool home in Kenton. It was one of those days when the thunderheads bloom in the afternoon sky but never drop any rain. Bud was not well, but this old cowpuncher kept a cigarette dangling from his lips and his mind was a history book of names, dates and deeds passed down by his family. His great-grandfathers came to the region about the end of the Civil War; both of his grandfathers grew up ranching near Kenton in what was known as No Man's Land.

"My great-grandfather Jones came out in 1865 and was ranching when he went to town one day and nobody ever saw him again. My grandfather, when he was nine, worked on a freight wagon to Ft. Worth where he had kinfolk. He was breaking horses when he was a teenager and moved to No Man's Land in 1875. Their ranch was just a few miles from here. He worked for seven years before the syndicate started selling things off. My other grandfather came in here and put together

200,000 acres. Great-granddad Davis once drove 2,000 head from Ft. Sumner to Pueblo, Colorado. When they got into rough country, one cowboy told my great-granddad, 'Bud, I don't think we have enough help to get through.'

"That evening four horsemen rode into camp and Bud shook hands. 'Look's like you need some help,' one of them said. 'We'll help you out for a couple of days if you feed us.'

"So they helped out and when the herd got near Raton where the country was smooth, they left, telling Bud: 'Well, you're in pretty good country. We got a job up north and that's where we're headed.'

"Well, my great-granddad knew who they were. It was Butch Cassidy and the Sundance Kid and some of their gang. That was about 1881 when the train out of Virginia City was robbed in Las Vegas. Don't know how many millions of gold they got.

"My great-grandmother, she had a boarding house in Ft. Sumner. Mary Ann Meghera was her name. Another outlaw, Billy the Kid, ate there and he had one place at the table to sit and if it was taken he said nothing but would go away and then come back when it was vacant. He could see all around from his table. She said there wasn't a nicer gentleman than that fellow, but he was a booger with the six-shooter."

Bud glanced out the kitchen window towards Black Mesa, a long ridge riding the north horizon. The Mesa is covered with cholla and cactus, mesquite and juniper. It is a dry summer and the puddle ponds have dried up, exposing their bleached and cracked bottoms. The mesa is, at 4,973 feet, the highest point in Oklahoma. From the bluffs the basin where dinosaur tracks are laid down in ossified mud is visible, as is Carrizo Creek, where a posse hanged eleven outlaws from the Coe gang. Sometimes it is fact and fiction that make up history in this country of violent folklore, hidden treasure and western mythology. It is a toss-up in what to believe.

Bud's mind went back to a day he spent cowpunching on the ridge in the 1930s.

"My brother-in-law and I, we was out on Black Mesa checking water and looking for cattle. We rode up the mesa and looked north and we saw the blackest rain clouds. We kept riding and about noon I said to Jimmy that they weren't rain clouds. It looked like dynamite had blown on the ground and the black dust was curling and billowing towards us. We started to head for home when it hit us.

"The horses, they just quit on us, stopped dead. We pulled our shirttails over our heads, took the bridles and saddles off and decided to wait out the dust. Then it kind of broke and we walked our horses and we ran on a fence and I hit it and there was nothing but a ball of fire running up and down the wire. We sat down, not daring to move and then the clouds broke and we could see a road and we got home about 11:00 at night. The windmill was spinning wildly and the first thing I done was shut it off and when I pulled the lever it shot fire for a quarter of a mile. That dust was so charged I didn't ever again fool with it."

Bud went off to war and when he came back he married and had two girls. Then he lost his first wife in a car accident. Wages went up and so did the price of land, from $1.00 an acre in the 1930s to $176 an acre – if you care to buy 3,000 acres.

Bud has a bad cough but keeps the cigarette in his mouth and starts to talk about the 200 pound hailstone that fell through a neighbor's roof.

Mildred, Bud's second wife, called to say Bud died on January 4, 1996.

The construction for Optima Lake, which sits dry in the middle of the panhandle near Hardesty, was authorized by Congress in 1937. Construction began in 1966 and the dam was completed 12 years later. Who knows why, perhaps it was the weather change, or just plain stupidity on the part of the Corps of Engineers but the lake never filled...$47 million down the drain.

Glenn Muir and his cat Tom live a few miles away in a trailer on a section of the OJ Ranch. Glenn is in his late 70s, tall, handsome, and, well, tough. Years ago he belonged to a street gang in Sacramento. He was a tailor, fought his way through Europe during World War II and began cowpunching in Colorado. He was never shot but once, and that was in Oklahoma.

"Who shot you?"

"Well, they was revenuers and I was smuggling."

"How come they did that?"

"Well, they shot me first."

Glenn is sitting in his living room, chewing tobacco. A picture of his mother and John Wayne are on the wall, as is a hand-colored triptych of Yosemite that looks about 100 years old. There is a weed-whacker on the dining table. Spurs hang on the wall and a grasshopper passes time on the lamp without a shade. The couch is a bed. Tom the cat wanders in.

"A rattlesnake got that cat in the yard. Tom come in at night, all swelled up in the paw and chest. Well, I put some coal oil on it and let him go...thought I was going to be rid of him but the swelling went down."

Tom makes a nuisance of himself.

"TOM, NOW YOU GIT DOWN FROM THERE!"

SLAP goes the fly swatter. Tom scurries off but is back in a couple of minutes, making more mischief.

"Now that lake, it's a real sore spot with the people. It ain't no lake, but a mud hole. We don't get the flash floods anymore where you see cottonwoods and dead cattle float by. We got the Beaver River and across another meadow is the Palo Duro. If they built that dam right here it would have worked.

"They moved people off their land to build that lake. In my opinion they made a big mistake. You know, stupidity. The big boys, they sit up in Oklahoma City. Hell, they don't know anything about this country."

Glenn's body aches with so many years in the saddle. He swears he never will drive a three wheeler, which has made horses obsolete on this ranch. He was married once but prefers to live alone.

"You know, some young people in gangs come out here from Hardesty. They like to fool around."

Then he gives a little smile.

"They think they're tough, but they wouldn't make a wart on a tough man's chest."

The Elephant Saloon can thank its short, violent and bawdy existence to what was known as The Strip – land between the 100 and 103rd meridian south of Liberal, Kansas. No Man's Land they called it, for there was no government and no law. In 1888 the Santa Fe Company put in a rail head a few miles west of Liberal to ship cattle from the Strip. Cowboys, after a long cattle drive, craved a wild weekend and, as Kansas was dry, it did not take long for Beer City to spring up in No Man's Land, within rifle shot of Liberal. It became a town of bars and brothels, gamblers and smugglers, thieves and cutthroats, pimps and panderers. The town was never laid out and grew around stacks of beer barrels and hooch brought in from the Hog Creek still.

The Elephant Saloon was a leading establishment. The story of Beer City was recounted by Harry E. Chrisman in his well–written book *Lost Trails of the Cimarron* (Sage Books, Denver, 1961).

According to Chrisman's book, a fellow by the name of Brushy Bush elected himself Marshall. He kept the town in line with his six-shooter and a sawed-off shotgun; his main interest was bullying people and shaking down the saloons.

Two young men, Joe Low and Dee Hannah, were selected for a prize fight to be followed by a Grand Masked Ball. Pussy Cat Nell, a local madam – legend says she worked out of the Elephant Saloon – was collecting bets. Brushy demanded 5% of the stake and when Pussy Cat put up a fuss, he beat upon her face with the butt of his six-shooter.

A week later Pussy Cat was sitting in her room when she saw Brushy walking the street. She grabbed the double-barreled shotgun she kept loaded with Blue Whistlers (a local term for buckshot), aimed the gun out the window and gave Brushy both barrels.

That did him in. Other folks took up the cause and shot up what was left of Brushy. People who buried him said he was so full of holes his body lifted like a sack of corn meal.

Chrisman, who found this story, called Beer City the Sodom and Gomorrah of the Plains. It was also known as the Queen City of the Southwest Cattle Land and Sin City. When the Panhandle became part of Oklahoma Territory in 1890, and law and order rode into town, Beer City quickly ended its two-year-life.

"They just carted the town off," says Bob Hood. Bob is a local rancher on whose land was built Tent City – also known as White City. It existed during the Beer City era. Tent City never became popular as it was downwind from the stock pens where cattle were loaded onto the trains.

"Some buildings were torn down and the boards were used on other structures in Liberal," Bob said. "Some were lifted up and moved whole."

Alvin Matkin now owns the land where Beer City once stood. When he reshaped the field for crops by burying Main Street under 10 feet of soil, he found a human leg bone. Bob Hood unearthed other human bones when he was plowing one of his nearby fields. Perhaps one of them is all that remains of Brushy.

"I've been a soldier, chief engineer, head of a design department, a machinist. I have a degree in mechanical engineering and I worked for large and small corporations. I've been a crop duster and a bush pilot in Alaska, where I found I didn't know much about flying. I've lived all over the world and been in every state. My Dad was a Colonel in the Army and me, I'm an Army brat. Daddy said they are thieves, liars, whores and ministers in this world and there's no difference. I don't know what he had against whores."

Brian McDaniels was flying over the Oklahoma panhandle and decided, after looking down, that it was beautiful place to live. So he bought three lots in Kenton and set up $50,000 worth of machine tools.

People in Kenton, population 23, do not always appreciate outsiders. One rancher, at Kenton's town meeting, stated the town did not want any new businesses, and no newcomers.

Brian stood up and retorted, "I fought in Vietnam to protect you. I came here and bought my land and all this machinery and hope to make a living. You are a fourth generation here, you didn't go into the military, you get the state or the government to give you land to use at a cheap price and I can't come here and try to make a living?"

Brian recounted the story over a cup of coffee in his cramped living quarters next to his machine shop.

"I can appreciate them wanting to keep outsiders out as I've seen what happened in so many areas. If it is pretty it will be developed and then overdeveloped."

Brian is now a gunsmith, a trade he picked up from a Cajun rifle master. He recently designed two long range elk rifles, named for the local hills – the .338 and .375 Black Mesa Express. He creates the cartridges and the rifles, which he custom makes in his machine shop. He demonstrates the rifles to customers by stepping outside, taking a prone position and aiming his rifle at a rock 1000 yards away. He then pulverizes it.

Brian is not reticent about his views on firearms but he looks at rifles as an art form as much as a weapon.

"A gun is good protection until we get back the standards we dropped so much. We have to bring back pride in what we do and develop respect. The Surgeon General says we need safe guns and bullets. What are we supposed to do, put a condom over them?

"Yes, my gun can kill but it is not designed for that. I take pride in my craft, my workmanship and the quality I do, in the woodworking, the welding, the machinery work and the art of it."

Brian drinks coffee continually and smokes about as much. His mind never seems to take a break except when he cradles the Black Mesa in his arms. Then you would think he is holding his baby, the way he smiles.

"I take great satisfaction in this rifle. I've found something I have worked for all my life, something good."

Dia Webb's dream is to move from Boise City to New York City and perform on Broadway, singing or dancing.

Dia was a vocal and performance major at Oklahoma Baptist University, with a minor in theater and piano. She, her father and mother sing at revivals and country churches. Mom sings alto and plays the piano, Dia sings soprano, and Dad is the tenor. When she is not in school Dia works at Wild Bill's RV, the family owned campsite, and makes slush cones for the kids who drop by to play miniature golf.

In 1992 Dia won newcomer talent in the Miss Oklahoma contest and received $2,500. She believes winning Miss Oklahoma or Miss America would lead to a glamorous life in Manhattan. It is a dream and a hope that puts a smile on her face and a shine in her eyes.

"This year, well, I blew my Miss Oklahoma interview. I won my talent night and I guess I did all right in swimsuit and gown – they count for 15% each of the votes – but I muffed my interview in front of eight judges. You see, they ask you to introduce yourself, and talk about your critical issue."

Dia's critical issue is the importance of the two-parent family, the prevalence of divorce and what it does to children.

Although Dia lives in town, her family ran the Strong Ranch 15 miles west of Boise City where legend says there is a buried treasure of gold. She learned to ride, brand cattle and rope. Her horse Jesse is still out there. "Jesse, she's wild now," she says. She seems wistful to lose that part of her life.

"I'll miss Oklahoma when I leave," she says, as if this was her last day in Boise City. "Sometimes I feel I want to raise a family and live in a small town."

Even if Dia does not win Miss America, she swears she will still move to New York.

In the late afternoon the oxygen seems wrung out of the air. Thunder rumbles and the grain tower turns a ghostly pale white against a green-black sky. Two miles west of town a dust storm stops in its track and, as if ready to strike, masses into a spiral and begins twirling like a top. Above it gray black clouds are swirling and a barb like a scorpion's tail twirls down to meet the dust swirl. The tornado siren wails as sheets of rain quickly turn to hail. Then the tornado-in-the-making evaporates like a melting slush cone.

"I love it here, when it gets cloudy and the sky turns green," Dia says, when the sun again sparkles. She was wearing her Miss Oklahoma T-shirt.

The following year, in Atlantic City, Miss Oklahoma was indeed chosen as Miss America, but it was not Dia Webb.

Texas

It is 7:30 a.m. and you know the day is going to fry and Stanley Marsh III, followed by his driver, walks hurriedly out to Cadillac Ranch, the popular work of art he financed which is half-buried in a field outside of Amarillo.

"I ONLY GOT FIFTEEN MINUTES," he shouts and for the next fifteen minutes he makes the most of it.

"YESTERDAY I SAW THE NEW WYATT EARP FILM AND THEN I RENTED 'TOMBSTONE' WHICH IS A BLOODY SHOOT 'EM UP, BUT IN BOTH OF THEM THEY HAVE WYATT EARP MOVING FROM MISSOURI TO ARKANSAS TO ARIZONA AND THEY NEVER CROSS THE PLAINS! THE MOVIE-MAKERS CAN'T HANDLE THE VASTNESS OF THE HORIZON LIKE THIS! IT IS ENORMOUS! IT IS IMPRESSIVE! IT IS WONDERFUL AND IT IS WHAT MAKES MEN FREE!

"IT IS PEOPLE WHO CROSSED THE PLAINS WHO GOT REAL BALLS AND REAL NUTS! FAR AS YOU CAN SEE THERE WAS NOTHING BUT FLAT. THAT'S WHAT MAKES PEOPLE BETTER WHO LIVE ON THE PLAINS THAN PEOPLE WHO LIVE ON THE OCEAN! ONLY ABOUT 8% OF THE PEOPLE OF THE UNITED STATES LIVE AT LEAST 1,000 MILES AWAY FROM ONE OF THE GREAT LAKES OR GREAT OCEANS AND THOSE ARE THE ONLY 8% WHO COUNT AND THE REST YOU CAN JUST FLUSH INTO THE OCEAN. THOSE WHO LIVE OUT WHERE IT IS FLAT ARE GOD'S CHOSEN PEOPLE BECAUSE IF GOD WANTED PEOPLE TO LIVE NEAR THE OCEAN HE WOULD HAVE GIVEN THEM GILLS.

"TOM MIX WAS AT WYATT EARP'S FUNERAL AND YOU KNOW HE CRIED AT IT BECAUSE THEY WERE BURYING HIM IN CALIFORNIA AND NOT IN THE GREAT PLAINS, THAT'S WHY HE WAS CRYING.

"THE REALLY GOOD COWBOYS COME FROM THE HIGH PLAINS OF TEXAS. THE BIGNESS EXPANDED THEIR MINDS AND IT IS WHY WE SAY 'A MAN IS GOT TO DO WHAT A MAN IS GOT TO DO.'

"DO YOU THINK THE CADILLAC RANCH IS THE BEST THING YOU EVER SAW IN AMERICA?"

"They're great."

"DO YOU THINK THE CADILLAC RANCH IS THE BEST THING YOU EVER SAW IN AMERICA?"

"Yes!"

"THANKYA" he answers.

Stanley Marsh III drives away in a Continental.

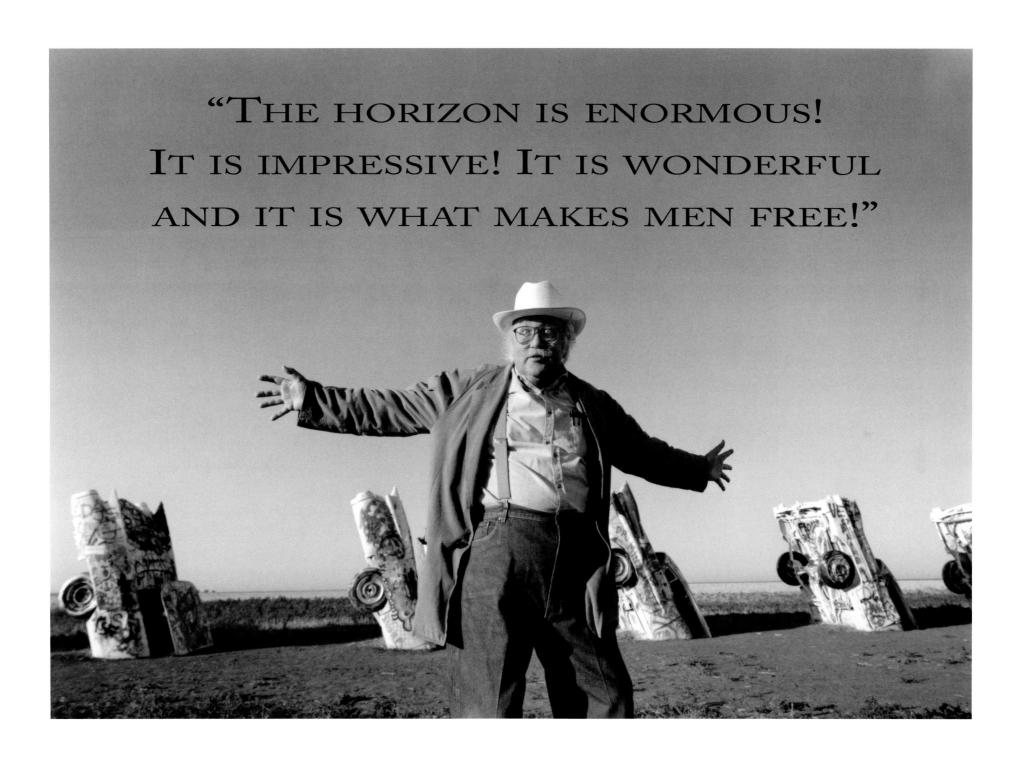

"THE HORIZON IS ENORMOUS!
IT IS IMPRESSIVE! IT IS WONDERFUL
AND IT IS WHAT MAKES MEN FREE!"

J.B. is a poet by nature and has been a cowpuncher for 30 years, working from the Great Divide to Fort Worth. His legs are as curved as the girth of a quarter horse. He chews his words, chops them off and lets them loose with a cadence and accent as pungent as the smell of cattle and sweat-stained saddle leather.

"Being a cowboy, well you can't explain it, it's a way of life, the way you treat other people, the way you work with them. It's a society with its own rules, its own etiquette," says J.B.

"We came across this country to escape from a rigid society," continues J.B. "Lot of us are Scots — they are people used to being free and don't care for rules. Many cowboys were black. They came for the same reason."

J.B. is from Whiteface, in the Texas panhandle. He says Texan cowboys have a style all their own.

"We're more utilitarian, more rough and rowdy and are on the practical end of it. A bunch of us went up to Arizona once to work with them buckaroo boys and heck, we could have gathered three pastures while they was still dressing their horses. Still, they have the same kind of outlook on life and the way it ought to be lived – family, work ethic, you know. A cowboy will cowpunch 'til he can't do it anymore."

"Roundup in the Spring" is an old cowboy poem, originally written by Carl Copeland and Jack Williams. It is a tradition of cowboy poetry for poets to recite or sing an old favorite in their own style, and sometimes add a couple of lines. This is J.B.'s version. "Roundup" is included in an audio tape he made called *Treasures*, which also includes his own poems.

Roundup In The Spring

In the lobby of a big hotel in New York Town one day
Set a bunch of fellers spinnin' yarns to pass the time away
They spoke of all the things they'd done and differnt sights they'd seen
Some of 'em praised Chicago town and others New Orleans

In the corner in an old armchair sat a man whose hair was gray
And he would listen eagerly to what they had to say
And I asked 'im where he'd like to be and heard that old voice ring
"I'd like to be in Texas, for the roundup in the spring."

They all sat still and listened to ever word he had to say
They knew that feller sitting there had once been wild and gay
They asked 'im for a story of his life out on the Plains
He slowly removed his hat and quietly began

Why I've seen 'em stompede oer them hills till you'd think they'd never stop
I seen 'em run for miles and miles, till their leaders dropped
I was foreman on a cow ranch, that's the callin' of a king
And I'd like to be in Texas, for the roundup in the spring

There's a grave in sunny Texas, where Josie Bridwell sleeps
There's a grove of leafy cottonwoods, her constant vigil keeps
In my heart's recollection of those carefree, bygone days
We rode the range together like two skippin' kids at play

Her gentle voice would call me in the watches of the night
I hear her laughter freshenin' the dew of early light.
But a fever took my darlin' on the day we were to wed
And left 'er cold and lifeless by the crossin' on the Red.

I see the cattle grazin' on the hills of early morn
See the campfire smokin' at the breakin of the dawn
Hear some cayuse neighin', I can hear the nightguard sing
I'd like to be in Texas, for the roundup in the spring.

"A cowboy
ain't a rancher!
Don't ever
forget that!"

More than 400 years ago Spanish priests pressed the first Texan wine. In 1914 a Texan became the first vintner to graft French vines to American roots. Now 26 vineyards produce over one million gallons throughout Texas. The best wine comes from the High Plains, where the loam, four to 13 feet deep, is sandy and the climate is warm and the nights are cool.

Cap*Rock Vineyards in Lubbock is aptly named as the Texas panhandle sits on a rock shelf on top of an immense mesa. Their new, five million dollar plant produces an outstanding cabernet, but their blush is more popular.

The company maintains 80 acres of chardonnay and cabernet vines in nearby Shallowater. The vineyard is surrounded by cotton fields serviced by whining irrigation pumps sucking up water. The vineyard is irrigated not by flooding the rows but with silent drips of water moistening individual vines.

The vineyard is kept in trim by the Cerda family. Pablo is the foreman and has 11 children ranging from 2 to 29 years. The entire field crew is related. The Cerdas were migrant workers; now they have lived in Texas for 15 years and are American citizens. Irma and Martha prune the vines and hope to graduate to better jobs, as did their sister, who is a computer programmer. Their brother Jesse works beside them. He has just entered college. He is known as Barkley for his passion for the basketball star. "I can do anything," he affirms. "I can be a basketball player. If I grow."

It is convection-oven hot in the vineyards where the Cerdas are pruning the vines. The soil is brick red and dry and coated with dust that puffs up when stepped on. In the distance, migrant workers, hoeing rows of cotton, flutter in heat waves against the horizon. Pruning vines on a June day during a Texan heat wave is work endured mostly in silence. The grapes, small and hard chartreuse-tinted balls, are bunched up tight to the stalk, as if they are seeking protection from the dizzy heat. Eventually the grapes will become heavy and soft and in the fall will be transformed into a blush, a cabernet or a flinty white, and most likely drunk by a well-dressed woman in a smoothly decorated, air-conditioned home or restaurant...probably in Austin or Dallas.

"*Rain or shine, we treat you fine,*" reads the business card of Becker Pump and Pipe. Bo Becker has been in the well business for 44 years and he and his son, Matt, service 2,400 wells. Bo is as hefty as Matt is skinny. They typify the Texans who live in the panhandle, on what is called the Staked Plains. They move faster, think swiftly, and have more than the average amount of Texan piss and vinegar. Bo also knows water like bankers know interest rates.

Bo: "Put two bankers in a barrel and roll them down a hill and they still come out sons-a-bitches."

Matt: "You say you come down from Oklahoma? Know what they call a pretty woman in Oklahoma?...A tourist!"

Me: "Know what they say in New Mexico about Texans? 'Poor, poor New Mexico. So far from God, so close to Texas.'"

They had to tell a couple of Yankee jokes before the conversation returned to water.

"It's a known fact that there is as much water on the earth as the day Christ walked around, but Atlas picks it up and drops it on this fifty and we don't have it no more. The water is here; it just gets moved around."

Bo sticks his hands in the bib of his overalls.

"That water table has been dropping for a long time," continues Bo. "In 1941, when we started irrigation, there were 6,000 big wells on the Great Plains. Now there are 96,000 in the High Plains in Texas. You know an eight-inch pump can dry up a lake in 36 hours?"

The last casing is put in, the motor is hooked up and the pump revs up to 3,450 and spins out the water, rust-colored at first then silver-clear – 80 gallons a minute from 160 feet down – a shallow well for these parts.

Cotton and wheat pay the bills for the Hintons, who are entering the fourth generation on their farm in Dougherty. The original Hintons who homesteaded the farm in the '20s, have died. Henry is semi-retired. His son, James, runs the farm with the help of his wife Sharon, a nurse. They have two children; son Matthew will, God willing, carry this farm into the 21st century. That is, if there is any water left.

According to Henry, during the 50s wells in this county were drilled about 250 feet until they tapped into the Ogallala aquifer. Now most wells are sunk about 350 feet. Drill another 50 feet and chances are the well comes up dry. Some wells are now abandoned and homes have run out of house water.

James is a "tech farmer." He could be an agronomist with his education, but prefers working a couple of sections and driving no more than 7,000 miles a year, including a trip to his wife's folks in Tennessee.

He protects the natural water – about 18 inches a year – by channeling it into a bulldozed lake and pumping it back to the fields. The lake was been dry in the last couple of years; the Texas sun can evaporate more water in a day than can be pumped out of the aquifer at 800 gallons a minute. The Hinton farm has a well that once pumped 1,000 gallons a minute, but is now down to a fourth of that and the aquifer is not being replenished.

In 1996, James wrote a letter just before this book was finished, which brought their life up to date:

...My family is doing fine. Sharon is now teaching a Certified Nurse's Aid course through a non-profit corporation we started last fall. I am trying to get fields prepared for planting next month along with taking care of our two children and caring for my cows that are currently calving. My parents are well. They are going to Colorado soon to visit grandkids.

The last two years have been very tough financially, due to reduced yields from lack of rain, severe insect infestation and a hail storm last June that wiped out everything. There were four tornadoes in that storm that covered a five-mile-wide swatch across us. Luckily, no one was injured and houses were not lost. That largest tornado was one-half mile in diameter when I found shelter. The National Weather Service Doppler maps showed that the tornado grew to one mile in diameter. We were without power for a day. The steel tower transmission line south of Dougherty had 19 structures toppled due to winds in excess of 200 mph, their engineered tolerance. I know how Dorothy felt in the "Wizard of Oz."

Currently, this is the seventh month without a precipitation event other than a couple of two-tenth-inch showers and a foggy day. The wheat that did emerge last fall is barely holding onto life. Hopefully, the rains will come this month. The rains always come, sometimes it's just a few days after we "think" it's too late, but out here rain is always welcome.

Two men were seated next to the barber shop on a bench shaded by the boardwalk. They were chatting and looking at nothing particular. Across the street is a vacant gas station and a false front covering up a number of empty, crumbling store buildings that no one wants to buy or rent. One of the men is Harold Ham, the barber for the town of Turkey.

Harold's father opened the barber shop in 1911. It was a two-seat shop which he later expanded to four. Harold began working in 1942 and fondly remembers the 50s when, on Friday night, every space on Main Street was filled with diagonally parked cars. Every shop was open and the town was as brightly-lit as a carnival. It was a lively scene; Harold has a photograph of it.

"We had families on the farm and come Friday night, they all came to shop, to eat, to dance. Well, there's no payroll anymore. The kid's have gone somewhere else. They're just old people here now."

One of the photographs hanging on his barbershop wall is of Harold cutting a child's hair. It is in color, beautifully lighted and is as saccharin as an old Saturday Evening Post cover. It was shot by a traveling German photographer. There are other photographs – of a football team, a baseball team, of a man standing on a scaffold, waiting to be hanged. The doomed man is a short fellow in a suit, his shoulders squared. A priest holds a cross and standing next to him is the ubiquitous official who wants his photograph taken – as if he knew instinctively that it would hang in a barber shop 85 years later.

"No, I don't know who that was they hanged, but it was our last public hanging. Took place in 1910. The baseball team, they were before me. That football team – they are all dead except three. That man there," and he pointed to a glossy publicity photo – "that's Bob Wills."

Harold explains that before Wills and The Texas Playboys became a nationally-known country-western band, he was a barber who learned his trade in this barbershop. Now the biggest event in this part of the panhandle is Bob Wills day. Over 15,000 country music fans flock to Turkey for a weekend of music.

Harold is a social security barber. Although time is running out for him and the town, he stays open, cuts a customer or so a day for $5.00 a head but spends most of the time sitting on the boardwalk, chatting to friends, watching the street and waving to the few who pass by.

J.B. Reece is in the yard attacking weeds growing in his driveway near an old pickup. He lives on an aged farm east of Tahoka. A broken down windmill, the skeleton of a cottonwood behind the house and two stumps in the front, a rusted Farmall tractor, a battered outhouse – altogether five buildings and a heap of boards from one that was blown down constitute the farm, gnawed gray by wind and hail, snow and dust and overwhelmed by the vastness of the sky and fields. The farmhouse of silvered clapboards has a classic, lonely elegance in its structure.

J.B. looks down at an anthill in his driveway.

"Got to get after that. They bite hard." He points towards a spot on his forearm.

"Put Clorox on it. It goes in deep and takes the sting away."

His hat is spotless and his clothes are freshly pressed and his fingernails are full, clean and shaped like a city lawyer's. He says he is close to 80, and his eyes wander to the sky and to the ground.

"I was born in this house and it's just a little older than me. We have the sweetest land around here. Don't know why it is so sweet. We grew wheat, cotton, milo, maize, sorghum and Johnson grass. Hogs like Johnson grass.

"I've lived here two years alone now. Had three children. One girl, she passed away when she was 22," and he turns away and looks down at the hoe blade.

"Got a girl working in Tahoka and a boy in the oil fields. He's making good money.

"My wife, she passed away two years ago. Got cancer and it went straight up," and he taps his head.

"We were so close," and he crosses two fingers on his right hand and holds them up. Then he turns away again and looks towards the sky.

"My wife, I liked her so much I don't like to talk about her." He looks towards the house.

"I put the shingles on the roof in 1951. Went to get some new ones the other day..." He nods towards the pile of boards which was once a storage barn.

"Wind blew it down six weeks ago."

He looks at the trees.

"They just died. I don't know why. They just did."

Emily Winters drives 75 mph down a dirt road the color of a red fox. She slows as a dust storm chasing sage balls and bending the soapweed crosses the road, then turns west over a cattle guard. The ranch she and her husband lease near Dalhart is 22 sections, most of which is surrounded by a rim that acts as a natural barrier – they only need seven miles of cross fences. There is a windmill in front of the house, a grizzled wagon, cow pies, old license plates on the ground, a couple of pickups with cracked windows, some salt blocks, a corral and barn. Up on the rim, following a road with ruts 18 inches deep, there is not a tree in sight.

"This is all I know and I don't know much," admits Frank Winters, a fifth generation rancher. Emily is from Tennessee (but says she was born to be a Texan rancher). "When you're doing what you love it's kind of like being on vacation all the time. You're doing what you want to do, so why go on vacation and do what you don't want to do?" Frank says.

Frank went east only once, to Tennessee, when he married Emily.

"I never did know there was so much water, trees and people in the whole world! Well, the trees ran a close second to what I hated the most. You can't see nothing out there but trees three feet in front of you.

"The people are, I dunno, they're weird. They hang together and are all worried about impressing everybody – they can't impress anybody because they are so worried about impressing everybody. They can't be their own people and they got their vision so split up on so many things they don't know what direction they're going in. They got so many rules and regulations, and everyone goes by them. Out here, we do what we have to do. If it gets along with the rules, that's fine and if it don't,

who cares and that's fine too.

"You're talking about my parents," accuses Emily.

"Noooo...it's just that way. Texans are direct. When I went back there, people won't say, 'Your shoes are untied.' They'll try to hint around about it.

"I don't take hints. If you want me to take a hint, then you got to hit me in the face with a wet mop."

Ranching is not an easy way to make a living, particularly with cattle prices so low, but for ten years the couple have been at it.

"It's not that we are trying to make money and do things. I think its bred in us, we been here so long. We'll get out on a property and we can see for 40 miles. If you just go slow you go all day and you still ain't got anywhere. So you got to go fast or you don't never get anywhere, you know what I mean?" asks Frank.

"I like handling horses and cattle, and I like doing it right. There's a way, there's an art to handling cattle and horses and I love it. I love doing that and to do it the way I feel is right I have to do it for myself."

The high plains of eastern New Mexico lie flat as a windless sea. The grass is burnt close to the ground by drought and dust storms are easily swirled by the winds that scuttle in from the mountains to the west. Cattle are sprinkled like grains of pepper on this blond terrain. Thunder clouds pass above the horizon, but they never drop enough rain.

It is hot, so very hot at Chicosa Lake, near the town of Roy. Overhead a hawk circles, to the north a ranch teeters in a mirage and a quiet wind flows over the land, sucking away moisture.

There is no water in the lake; its bed is cracked and dry, white with alkali. Only on one edge is there a smudge of green. Stamped in the baked mud are coyote tracks. Chicosa Lake is a state park and there is a campground and a lodge, but rarely is it visited, since the lake dried up.

The lake has been dry for years, but it was not always just a dusty indent. Charlie Goodnight considered it one of the most reliable water sources in this section of New Mexico. Between 1866 and 1875 over 250,000 cattle bawled their way up the Goodnight and Loving Trail through 2,000 miles of Texan and New Mexican alkali dust on their way to market in Colorado, Wyoming and Kansas. Charlie Goodnight and his partner Oliver Loving founded the trail, which skirts Chicosa Lake, in 1866 to bypass the fierce Comanches and Kiowas of the Staked Plains in Texas. Unfortunately, this did not prevent Loving from being killed by Indians in 1867. The next year Goodnight brought Loving's body from New Mexico to Texas, pulled by six mules and escorted by Texan cowboys.

Charlie Goodnight is a Texan legend. He was an Indian fighter and cattleman; and his character was the basis for *Lonesome Dove*, written by Larry McMurtry. Along the Goodnight and Loving Trail techniques for cowboying a thirsty and wild herd of longhorns were developed. Here rattled the first chuck wagon, a portable kitchen and supply wagon – all invented by Goodnight. The code of the cowboy emerged along this trail.

Goodnight remembered these moments in his later years. They are etched on a sign near the chuck wagon next to the empty lodge bordering the once-full, Chicosa Lake, where Goodnight and his crew squatted and ate their dinner:

"Taking all in all, my life on the trail was the happiest part of it. I wish I could find ways to describe the companionship and loyalty of the men toward each other. It is beyond imagination. The cowboy of the old days is the most misunderstood man on earth. He was as brave and chivalrous as it is possible to be."

Andy Wilkinson is a great-great nephew of Charlie Goodnight. A former corporate financial officer who quit to become a poet of the Plains, Andy drives old cars with no air conditioning, partly because he wants to and partly because it is all he can afford. He lives in Lubbock, the largest city on the Great Plains.

A literate man, intense, with a bent for historical research and a political sense of wrong, Andy writes poems and sings about change and its effect on the Plains. Andy wrote a series of poems on Charlie Goodnight, collected in the book of the same name.

In 1916 Charlie Goodnight held what became known as The Last Buffalo Hunt at his ranch in the Palo Duro Canyon. It signified to many people the closing of the old west. Over 11,000 people showed up at the event. Wilkinson's poem *The Last Buffalo Hunt* describes the event as seen by his Grandmother:

> *I's goin' on thirteen, in nineteen-and-sixteen,*
> *A new world replacin' the old:*
> *Ranges took fences, the plows took the grasses,*
> *Cow-trails were taken by roads.*
> *Papa packed the Buick and Mama saw to it*
> *We dressed in our best Sunday clothes,*
> *Set out at daylight for old Colonel Goodnight's*
> *To watch the last hunt for buffalo*
> *"...We saw four old men Indians*
> *Dressed up like white men,*
> *Shooting their arrows from bows,*
> *Riding their ponies*
> *Like it wasn't only*
> *The last time they'd hunt the buffalo...*

Prairie Without Buffalo

...They were shot down for the merchants

Grass plowed for greed,

The prairie paved until no green could grow;

Now there's only dreamers searchin',

While the whole world needs

The grass, the prairie, and the buffalo

Only in your dreams you'll know

The world we should have saved

For the prairie without buffalo

Is the ocean without waves...

Of my four journeys to the Plains, three were made hauling a 1968 Airstream. I often unhitched the camper and would drive sometimes 100 miles in search of photographs and stories. The last trip took place in the winter, and I left the Airstream at home and slept in motels or in my tent.

Many of the people in the book I met by chance. By the end of the fourth trip there were 400 pages of notes and 400 rolls of exposed film. I recorded interviews and impressions on a small Sony recorder.

Most of the portraits were taken with a Mamiya 6 MF camera system. The lenses are sharp and contrasty and the portraits are enhanced by the negative size. This camera is unobtrusive, quiet and quick to use, an important factor when interviewing and photographing people.

Some portraits and scenics were taken with a Plaubel Pro-Shift. This camera captures a 2¼ by 3¼ inch image with an extreme wide angle lens. It was designed for architectural use and is no longer made.

The panoramics were shot with a Fuji 6x17 camera equipped with a fixed 110mm lens. It shoots a seven inch long strip of film.

I usually carried a Leica M6 35mm camera equipped with a 21mm lens. This camera was used when the light was poor and the action swift.

I used Ilford HP5 Plus for portraits and FP4 Plus for scenics. Most of the panoramics were made with the latter film, using an orange filter. Sometimes I found a lack of contrast between the land and sky which was solved in two ways – either by using a blue filter with the FP4 Plus, which made the sky lighter, or by using Konica infrared film. The film was developed in Sprint chemistry. Prints were made with Ilford Multigrade and Galerie paper.

The book was designed on a Macintosh, using QuarkXpress and Adobe Photoshop. The type is Adobe Caslon. The photographs are duotones and were scanned by The Stinehour Press. I set up a company to publish my books after major publishers turned them down. This is the second in a series of books on rural Americans. The first, *Vermont People*, was self-published in 1990.

Peter Miller

I Want to Go Home, Home to Vermont

Buffalo, South Dakota, September, 1993.

There has been a change to the weather. The wind that crosses these Plains has gentled and cooled. The grassland in this unusually verdant, rainy summer is burnished by the sun. There is a certain smell in the air and a subtle change in the color of the sky and in my bones I feel the music of September. For the first time in three months I am thinking of Vermont.

It is September, and I want to go home.

September in Vermont. A subtle fragrance of drying leaves and grass and corn chaff floats in the air. This fragrance, intense under the mid-day sun, is wicked away by the cool nights, and the air becomes crisp as a morning frost. By noon a languorous haze has softened the edges of fields and hills. The cicada's buzz has been silenced on these windless, warm days, but now, in an indiscernible distance, a partridge thumps the air with his wings. The beat hesitantly accelerates, holds steady and then slowly fades. A pause, and then from a distance floats the whine of a corn chopper. A yellow school bus climbs a dirt road.

It is time to go home to Vermont.

Time slows in September. I want to amble up the hill to the lone maple and lie under it and watch the sun shimmer gold between the leaves. I want to see the first swamp maple leaves turn red as blood, audacious against the green sugar maples. I want to experience the bite in the first frost and the slow tempo of the color descending the hills. I want to feel the curt winds that blow in so quickly, changing the hazy days to a sharpness that makes my blood surge before Indian summer returns.

I love Vermont in the fall. It is September and I want to go home.

I miss the awe of seeing so high above the first geese flying south, their excited conversation trailing behind them. September is a time of contemplation of the year passed, for then begins the season of death and renewal. There is peace in Vermont at this time of life. A nostalgic feeling of life lived, loved and gone wells up in me. It is a sweet feeling, a private feeling, in this September time.

Oh, I want to go home, home to Vermont.

I miss the coming of bird season, of walking over stone walls and following hidden brooks, the water speckled with sunlight as it flows through alder patches where the woodcock lay. I miss the excitement of seeing my dog on point and the feel of a well-balanced shotgun floating in my arms, following the whistle of woodcock wings. I miss walking up wooded hills to dying apple orchards guarded by brambles and discovering the hidden stone foundations. I miss the mystery of wondering who lived there, who planted the trees, who picked the apples, who they loved. I miss the sweet smell of fallen leaves, cured by frost and sun. I miss the private places I have within the woods and mowings of Vermont, hidden so far away. They are my magic.

My blood says, go home, Peter, you've been away too long. It is September.

That first fragrance of fall flows within me, a scent that is drawing me to Vermont. I want to go home. I want to head my car east. I want to see familiar hills and the steady pace of leaves changing. I want to be part of this ceremony of life and death, as the season flames before it folds into itself and the land lies bone clean and neat. I want to blend with Vermont and counterpoint the months. Languorous September. Vibrant, dying, October. Stark November, the land surrendered and at peace, bare and brown, waiting for snow. These are my months.

I have come to love the Plains, but I want to go home. Home to Vermont.